The Cheyenne in Plains Indian Trade Relations
1795–1840

JOSEPH JABLOW

The Cheyenne
in Plains Indian Trade Relations
1795–1840

Introduction to the Bison Book Edition
by Morris W. Foster

University of Nebraska Press
Lincoln and London

Introduction to the Bison Book Edition copyright © 1994 by the University of Nebraska Press
Manufactured in the United States of America.

First Bison Book printing: 1994
Most recent printing indicated by the last digit below:
10   9   8   7   6   5   4   3   2   1

Library of Congress Cataloging-in-Publication Data
Jablow, Joseph.
The Cheyenne in Plains Indian trade relations, 1795–1840 / Joseph Jablow; introduction to the Bison book edition by Morris W. Foster.
p.   cm.
Originally published: New York: J.J. Augustin, 1951, in series: Monographs of the American Ethnological Society; 19.
Includes bibliographical references and index.
ISBN 0-8032-7581-1 (pa)
1. Cheyenne Indians—Commerce.   2. Cheyenne Indians—Economic conditions.
3. Cheyenne Indians—History.   4. Fur trade—Great Plains—History.   5. Subsistence economy—Great Plains.
E99.C53J3   1994
381′.089′973—dc20
94-5482
CIP

Reprinted by arrangement with the University of Washington Press. Originally published in 1950 as Monograph 19 of the American Ethnological Society.

∞

INTRODUCTION

by Morris W. Foster

Scholarly studies have shaped our sense that the Native peoples who lived on the Great Plains shared a common culture and the same general forms of social organization—being more alike than they were different. Scholars have explained these similarities in different ways, but the common strategy of their writing about the Plains has always been the same: to generalize from "tribe" to region and then to use that regional identity as an explanation for tribally-specific features of social and cultural organization. This Euroamerican preference for regional characterizations and explanations of diversity has not been limited to academics.

Beginning with their earliest explorations of North America, Euroamericans have divided up and labeled its outwardly distinctive geographic regions. Some of those places named, such as Cibola, have proven illusory but others, like the Plains, have come to make up the primary conceptual framework through which the continent and the Native peoples who reside on it have been understood by subsequent generations of explorers, colonists, homesteaders, moviegoers, and academics. Anthropologists, for instance, divide the continent and its Native populations into geographically distinct "culture areas" to characterize its indigenous diversity while a movie screen filled with open grassland and bison causes an audience to expect the appearance of Indians on horseback. These expectations are based on the use of ecology and economy to index social and cultural identities. That use is part of a discursive pattern common to both popular and scholarly texts that has made the regional location of a Native people as ineluctable a part of their identity as the name by which they are known.

We readily recognize that the Plains was a physical landscape with ecological and economic consequences for the Native peoples who resided within it—but ignore the fact that it is also a historiographic landscape with consequences for how we understand the Native peoples who lived there before the grasslands were plowed under and the bison slaughtered.

Joseph Jablow's monograph, *The Cheyenne in Plains Indian Trade Relations 1795–1840,* is a significant feature in that historiographic landscape. Along with Bernard Mishkin's *Rank and Warfare among the Plains Indians* (1940) and Oscar Lewis' *The Effects of White Contact upon Blackfoot Culture, with Special Reference to the Role of the Fur Trade* (1942), Jablow's study furthered the argument that the economic consequences of European activities on the Plains transformed Native communities—so much so that the historic Plains must be considered a qualitatively different place from the prehistoric Plains. This view ran counter to that of more established scholars such as Wissler (1917, 1926) and Lowie (1916, 1927), then the dominant voices in the academic discourse about the Plains, who argued instead that the characteristic features of Plains social and cultural organization were already established when Europeans arrived and were only incrementally or quantitatively altered as a result of Native–Euroamerican interactions. This latter view has subsequently been promoted by scholars such as Eggan (1966) and Wood (1980) and, for reasons described below, remains the dominant position today.

As Mishkin had in describing the organizational consequences for Kiowas of surplus wealth from their trade with Euroamericans, Jablow took the Cheyennes as a test case of the extent to which Euroamerican trade became the driving force in Cheyennes' relations with other Native peoples on the Plains. Jablow demonstrated that competition for trading opportunities (both with Natives and with Euroamericans) was a successful explanation in accounting for what we know of Cheyenne history. Between 1750 and 1780, bands of previously horticultural Cheyennes came onto the northern Plains grasslands, probably from the Great Lakes area, to exploit the greater availability of horses and bison. By 1795, nomadic Cheyenne bands had become important elements in the trade networks that spanned the Plains region and extended into the Southwest, the Plateau, the Gulf Coast, and the Eastern Woodlands. The Cheyennes traded horses to the horticultural villagers of the Middle Missouri (the Mandan, Hidatsa, and Arikara) competing with various Siouian bands for the Euroamerican goods accessible through those village middlemen. With the decline of the Middle Missouri villages after 1800, though, Cheyenne bands took advantage of two different economic strategies, one emphasizing direct trade with Euroamerican agents on the northern Plains and the other emphasizing the greater availability of horses (mainly through raiding) on the southern Plains. This latter strategy resulted in competition and subsequent alliances with Kiowa, Apache, and Comanche bands. Cheyennes continued to exploit changing opportunities for trade through the Civil War, after which their economic contribution became less vital to the increasing Anglo-American presence throughout the Plains. Ultimately, they were confined to reservations in Oklahoma and Montana.

Working from this sequence of events, Jablow fashioned the thesis that intertribal and Indian–Euroamerican trade on the Plains was the dominant context within which Native social organizations were ordered, enabling production and exchange, alliance and warfare, centralized authority and individual enterprise, in short all of the classic features that Euroamerican texts have reified as traditional Plains life or culture. Jab-

low's monograph speaks about Cheyennes but directly addresses its
statements to those of other scholars such as Lowie, Wissler, Mishkin,
Smith, and Strong, who had created a particular idea of the Plains. For
that reason, Jablow's research consisted of reading eighteenth and nineteenth century accounts of Cheyennes and twentieth-century interpretations of those narratives. The work of Jablow's narrative is to construct an
account of the consequences of intertribal trade on the Plains that is con-
sistent with those historical and scholarly statements used as the authority for his own statements. Jablow did not visit existing Cheyenne communities for this study because those were, by the mid-twentieth century,
already thought to be outside the discourse about their own history. Consequently, while we learn a great deal about how Cheyennes have been
described and explained by non-Cheyennes, we learn relatively little
about the internal organization of their community or Cheyenne accounts of their shared identity. Instead, Jablow's study is about a textual
"Cheyenne" that existed on the pages of Euroamerican journals, reports,
and published descriptions between 1795 and 1840, explicated by the
equally textual idea of "the Plains" as elaborated by scholars some time
after the last nomadic bands of Native peoples had been confined to reservations.

I hasten to add that none of these absences is a fault in Jablow's text;
rather, they are characteristic of how we have represented the Plains and
its Native inhabitants. More recent studies of Cheyennes have attempted
to combine ethnographic fieldwork in contemporary communities with
ethnohistorical explanation (i.e., Moore 1987 and Schleisier 1987) but
even those efforts do not fully succeed in finding bases for continuity between pre-reservation and post-reservation communities that are not
specific to the distinctive combination of largely external conditions
which we recognize as the ideal Plains of both scholarly and popular
imagination.

The distinction between subsistence and trade activities that Jablow
discusses in his study is not well specified in the Plains literature, but it is
at the heart of the argument that the historic Plains differed fundamentally from the prehistoric Plains. It is difficult for someone living in an in-
dustrialized community to appreciate the idea of getting our everyday necessities for living from one kind of activity while obtaining our wealth
(that which denotes prestige, raises status, and confers power) from a different kind of activity. Instead, we provide for both the necessities and
wealth from the same source—participation in a capitalist economy. Native Plains communities, in contrast, participated in two economies: the
hunting, gathering, and sometimes horticultural economy that was indeed a carry-over from prehistoric times and the trading economy based
on European goods (primarily horses, firearms, and ammunition, but also

including metals and decorative items). On the northern Plains this latter economy was fueled by the supply of pelts generated by Native trappers while on the southern Plains it was fueled by horse raiding and, later
in time, cattle raiding.

In trying to explain the organization of Native communities, scholars
have focused either on the subsistence economy (using ecological explanations) or the trade economy (using economic explanations) but have
had difficulty in integrating the two except insofar as they have attempted to speculate on the ecological constraints of maintaining large
horse herds for purposes of trade. Such speculations, however, have taken
the form of statistical manipulations of highly questionable horse herd
estimates rather than of explanations of human conceptualizations and
actions (Osborne 1983, Bamforth 1988, Flores 1991). Native Plains peoples, however, had no such difficulties in integrating the two economies.
Cheyenne residence bands, military societies, political organization,
kinship, and religious ceremonies were all calculated in reference to
those dual material conditions of everyday life. Other, non-material dynamics were also at work in the organization of those communities. How
these different factors should be weighted in understanding the social
and cultural arrangements by which Native people ordered their lives on
the Plains is a long-standing question. Euroamerican scholars, though,
have tended to prefer reductionary explanations in representing the organization of Plains communities—the idea of a homogeneous Plains being the most reductionary and economic and ecological arguments being
the means through which complexity and diversity have been reduced to
parsimony and similarity. In his study, Jablow described the economic
bases of intertribal relations but stopped short of constructing a broadly
deterministic Plains model based on his Cheyenne example. Thus, his
monograph is a very suggestive statement of what remains today an un-
resolved problem in understanding the pre-reservation organization of
Native Plains communities.

Curiously, the economic analysis that Jablow published in 1950 is still
fresh and worth reprinting today while other contemporaneous studies of
the Plains are now dated by subsequent texts. Jablow's underused economic conception of the Plains region continues to challenge the ecological conception that has dominated the Plains discourse both then and
now. The relative neglect of economic explanation has been mainly for institutional rather than intellectual reasons. As social actions, scholarly
texts are oriented to institutional features of the academic world. For
most of the four decades since its publication, Jablow's economic thesis
has been out of fashion in the small segment of that world interested in
the Plains.

Since World War II there has been a marked increase in attention to

Plains archaeology at the same time as there has been a sharp decrease in attention to Plains ethnology. Beginning with WPA excavations in the 1930s and continuing with extensive excavations funded by the Corps of Engineers and mandated by new federal laws in subsequent decades, Plains archaeology has boomed. There are, today, hundreds of practicing archaeologists working on the Plains excavating and analyzing prehistoric human occupations. In contrast, the most active period of ethnological investigation of Plains communities occurred in the first third of the twentieth century. Subsequently, funding for fieldwork outside North America became more readily available than funding for work in communities within the continent. As a result, only a few dozen ethnologists still actively research Plains peoples.

The larger contingent of Plains archaeologists whose interests have dominated Plains studies in the last fifty years has generally favored ecological over economic explanations of historic Plains social organization because the ecological models are more easily used as analogies for interpreting archaeological information. Indeed, economic explanations of the kind developed by Jablow treat Euroamerican trade as a fundamental transformation of the indigenous Plains from precontact times—hardly a model usable for archaeological purposes. The influence of larger numbers of archaeologists and the significance of the external funding they brought into universities in the postwar period as anthropology departments were growing, adding more faculty and producing more graduates than before the war, resulted in a bias in favor of the ecological idea of the Plains. The cohort of Columbia graduates influenced by W. Duncan Strong whose Plains monographs offered an alternative perspective on the region published their studies in the 1940s and 1950s but taught in smaller, less prominent departments primarily on the East Coast. Jablow, for instance, spent the bulk of his academic career at Brooklyn College. Significantly, only one of the advocates of the competing economic view obtained a position in an anthropology department with a prominent graduate research program on the Plains—and his monograph was not published until long after he had been hired and gained tenure (e.g., Holder 1970).

Other than their differential utility as archaeological explanations, however, ecological models have been used in much the same manner as have economic models to construct a singular idea of Native Plains social and cultural organization. The classic statement of Plains ecology was Symmes Oliver's 1962 monograph, *Ecology and Cultural Continuity as Contributing Factors in the Social Organization of Plains Indians,* though ecological conceptions of the Plains region have had a long history of both popular and scholarly textual statements. Oliver attempted to identify "true" Plains tribes and to explain those whose social and cultural organization appeared to vary from a core set of common features. Like his predecessors, Oliver concluded that a regional concept of the Plains shaped the Native peoples who moved about it rather than the other way around.

Economic arguments, however, are now becoming more prominent in discussions of the historic Plains. A recent article by Patricia Albers (1993) is, in many ways, an update on Jablow's intertribal thesis. Albers (1993:97–100) argues that Plains intertribal relations were of three kinds: warfare (competition), symbiosis (complementarity), and merger (cooperation). In Albers' view, these three forms of interdependence arose from different conditions affecting the organization and distribution of production and exchange on the Plains. Symbiosis was the result of different labor specializations among geographically contiguous populations, such as bison hunting and agriculture, while warfare was the result of two contiguous populations competing in the same specialization, such as a trading speciality like supplying horses. Merger, in Albers' scheme, was also a consequence of parallel specialization in the same territory but in a situation in which cooperation against other, external populations was preferable to competition within that territory.

Albers conceptualizes the eighteenth-century Plains region as comprised of alliance chains running from north to south with contiguous links of the same chain basing their relations on symbiosis and contiguous links of competing chains basing their relations on warfare. Thus, Cheyennes had symbiotic relationships with Kiowas because the latter traded horses from the South while the former traded goods obtained from the British in the North, most significantly firearms (Jablow 1950:59). In contrast, Cheyennes had more hostile relations with Tetons because both competed for trade opportunities with Arikara villagers (Jablow 1950:56–57). As Euroamerican middlemen increasingly penetrated the interior of the Plains during the nineteenth century, those chains broke as Euroamerican goods became more directly accessible. During this period, merger became a more common strategy than symbiosis because external Anglo-American populations began to compete directly with Native hunters and traders. Thus, northern Cheyennes entered into cooperative relationships with various Siouian divisions, including the Teton, and southern Cheyennes cooperated with Arapahos, Comanches, Kiowas, and Plains Apaches during the immediate prereservation period.

Albers' classification of Plains intertribal relations is a more formal and explicitly materialist framework than was Jablow's. She also goes much further than did Jablow in emphasizing the homogeneous idea of the Plains over the diversity of Native cultural or ethnic identities. Albers (1993:129–30) argues that there was a plasticity of cultural or ethnic identity on the nineteenth-century Plains as populations flowed from one social unit to another in response to changes in the interdependent material conditions of the larger regional political economy:

> In the historic Plains, patterns of interdependence, alliance making, and exchange were not always defined nor differentiated along exclusively ethnic lines. Symbiotic ties, with their attending specializations in production and/or distribution, were established between groups from differing tribes as well as among those of the same tribe. While members of one tribe often competed with people from tribes other than their own, hostility and warfare could erupt within the body politic of a single tribe, leading to internal fissioning and eventual separation. Conversely, while coresidency and territorial sharing linked people of the same tribal origin in a merger relationship, they could also join groups of differing ethnic backgrounds. The dynamic processes which united and divided populations along single as well as multitribal lines were the same because they were constituted in shared institutional frameworks of kinship and sodality.

This is the idea of the Plains with a vengeance. Distinct identities as expressed in differing languages, belief systems, and other cultural markers are immaterial to regional political economic processes. Nor does Albers (1993:131) make any distinction between internal and external social relations and arrangements. Instead, she characterizes all those relations as cut from the same cloth of kinship and sodality. In her model of the Plains, the shifting conditions of the regional political economy caused Native peoples to move among changing social units with essentially interchangeable ethnic or cultural identities.

While Albers' particular view of intertribal Plains relations derives from her historical materialist perspective, a theory used by only a few other Plains scholars (e.g., Klein 1977, 1980 and Moore, 1974, 1982, 1987), the way in which she constructs her arguments is a piece with previous texts about the Plains upon which her statements depend. Indeed, for all of Albers' protestations of a materialist analysis, her method at bottom is a textual one. Each citation she provides to exemplify her case for the Plains as a formative political economy is to a prior academic study, not to primary historical accounts of Plains peoples. Consequently, her conclusions are based on the conclusions of other academic studies that are, in the case of Jablow whom she cites frequently in support of her ideas, based in part on the conclusions of still other academic studies. Much of the authority for her conception of the Plains has gone through at least two prior discursive uses from an initial contemporaneous observation in some historical text that was itself a product of the ongoing discourse about the Plains.

Albers' conclusion that the Plains is the only enduring reality while individual tribal identities are more ephemeral epiphenomena is a result of this textual interdependence. By relying almost exclusively on scholarly interpretations of historical statements as the evidence for her claims, Albers' conclusions are derived from examples that already have been organized according to the idea of the Plains. Had she relied instead on primary historical observations, the result would have been less certain because those comprise a more dispersed set of statements that, unlike academic texts, were not uniformly subjected to as strong a version or dogma of the centrality of the Plains concept. Thus, Albers takes the scholarly image of Plains Indians to the same level of generality as the popular image. The irony is that, for all Albers writes about the transience of cultural or ethnic identity on the Plains, her argument repeatedly invokes the concept of discrete "tribes" and unified identities such as Cheyenne, Comanche, and Teton. Given the dependence of her text on prior texts, including Jablow's, there is simply no other way to phrase her statements. On the other hand, Jablow's study, because it depends in part on primary historical accounts of Cheyennes, is less dismissive of the significance of such Native identities.

After more than four centuries we are still finding our way on the Plains. And it is now reasonable to ask whether we should treat the region as the controlling context within which its constituent units (high plains, prairies, riverine valleys, Cheyennes, Kiowa, and Comanches, etc.) are best understood. As the contrast between Albers and Jablow shows, though, we are even uncertain about the reality and definition of those units. Thus, it is important to continue to read works like Jablow's to appreciate how far we have traveled and in what manner we have arrived at the present point in our accumulated knowledge about the part of North America and its Native peoples. In part because of this continuing journey, the Plains will no doubt remain an idea of some fascination for Euroamericans.

REFERENCES CITED

Albers, Patricia. 1988. Symbiosis, Merger, and War: Contrasting Forms of Intertribal Relationship among Historic Plains Indians. In *The Political Economy of North American Indians,* cited by John H. Moore. Norman: University of Oklahoma Press.

Albers, Patricia and William James. 1986. Historical Materialism vs. Evolutionary Ecology: A Methodological Note on Horse Distribution and American Plains Indians. *Critique of Anthropology* 6(1):87–100.

———. 1991. Horses without People: A Critique of Neoclassical Ecology. In *Explorations in Political Economy: Essays in Criticism,* edited by R.K. Kanth and E.K. Hunt. Savage, Md.: Rowman and Littlefield Publishers, Inc.

Bamforth, Douglas. 1988. *Ecology and Human Organization on the Great Plains.* New York: Plenum Press.

Benedict, Ruth. 1932. Configurations of Culture in North America. *American Anthropologist* 34:1–27.

Blakeslee, Donald J. The Plains Interband Trade System: An Ethnohistoric and Archaeological Investigation. Ph.D. diss. University of Wisconsin–Milwaukee. University Microfilms, 1975.

Driver, Harold E. 1961. *Indians of North America.* Chicago: University of Chicago Press.

Driver, Harold E. and J. L. Coffin. 1975. Classification and Development of North American Indian Cultures: A Statistical Analysis of the Driver-Massey Sample. *Transactions of the American Philosophical Society* 65(3).

Eggan, Fred. 1966. *The American Indian: Perspectives for the Study of Social Change.* Chicago: Aldine.

Ewers, John C. 1955. *The Horse in Blackfoot Indian Culture: With Comparative Materials from Other Tribes.* Bureau of American Ethnology, Bulletin 159. Washington, D.C.: Government Printing Office.

Farrand, L. 1904. *The Basis of American History: 1500–1900.* New York: Frederick Ungar Publishing Co.

Flores, Dan. 1991. Bison Ecology and Bison Diplomacy: The Southern Plains from 1800 to 1850. *Journal of American History* 78(2):465–83.

Foster, Morris W. 1992. Introduction to *Rank and Warfare among the Plains Indians* by Bernard Mishkin. Lincoln: University of Nebraska Press.

Holder, Preston. 1970. *The Hoe and the Horse on the Plains.* Lincoln: University of Nebraska Press.

Holmes, W.H. 1903. Classification and Arrangement of the Exhibits of an Anthropological Museum. Annual Report of the Smithsonian Institution for 1901. Washington, D.C.: Government Printing Office.

Klein, Alan M. 1977. Adaptive Strategies and Process on the Plains: The Nineteenth Century Cultural Sink. Ph.D. diss., State University of New York at Buffalo.

———. 1980. Plains Economic Analysis: The Marxist Complement. In *Anthropology on the Great Plains,* edited by W. Raymond Wood and Margot Liberty. Lincoln: University of Nebraska Press.

Kroeber, Alfred L. 1939. Cultural and Natural Areas of Native North America. University of California Publications in American Archaeology and Ethnology 38.

Lewis, Oscar. 1942. *The Effects of White Contact on Blackfoot Culture, with Special Reference to the Role of the Fur Trade.* American Ethnological Society Monograph 6.

Lowie, Robert. 1916. Plains Indian Age-Grade Societies: Historical and Comparative Summaries. American Museum of Natural History Anthropological Papers 11:877–992.

———. 1927. Origin of the State. New York: Harcourt Brace.

———. 1954. Indians of the Plains. New York: American Museum of Natural History.

Mason, O.T. 1896. The Influence of Environment upon Human Industries and

Arts. Annual Report of the Smithsonian Institution for 1895. Washington, D.C.: Government Printing Office.

Mishkin, Bernard. 1940. *Rank and Warfare among the Plains Indians*. American Ethnological Society Monograph 3.

Moore, John H. 1974. Cheyenne Political History, 1829–1894. *Ethnohistory* 21(4):329–59.

———. 1982. The Dynamics of Scale in Plains Indian Ethnohistory. Papers in Anthropology 23(2):225–46.

———. 1987. *The Cheyenne Nation: A Social and Demographic History*. Lincoln and London: University of Nebraska Press.

Oliver, Symmes C. 1962. Ecology and Cultural Continuity as Contributing Factors in the Social Organization of Plains Indians. *University of California Publications in American Archaeology and Ethnology* 43:1–90.

Osborn, Alan J. 1983. Ecological Aspects of Equestrian Adaptations in Aboriginal North America. *American Anthropologist* 85:563–91.

Roe, Frank G. 1955. *The Indian and the Horse*. Norman: University of Oklahoma Press.

Schlesier, Karl H. 1987. *The Wolves of Heaven: Cheyenne Shamanism, Ceremonies, and Prehistoric Origins*. Norman: University of Oklahoma Press.

Secoy, Frank R. 1953. *Changing Military Patterns on the Great Plains*. American Ethnological Society Monograph 21.

Smith, Marian W. 1938. The War Complex of the Plains Indians. Proceedings of the American Philosophical Society 78.

Spier, Leslie. 1921. The Sun Dance of the Plains Indians: Its Development and Diffusion. American Museum of Natural History Anthropological Papers 16:451–527.

Strong, W. Duncan. The Plains Culture Area in the Light of Archaeology. *American Anthropologist* 35:271–87.

Vehik, Susan C. 1988. Late Prehistoric Exchange on the Southern Plains and its Periphery. *Midcontinental Journal of Archaeology* 13(1):41–68.

Webb, Walter Prescott. 1932. *The Great Plains*. New York: Grosset and Dunlap.

Wilson, Clyde. 1963. An Inquiry into the Nature of Plains Indian Culture Development. *American Anthropologist* 65:335–69.

Wissler, Clarke. 1906. *Diffusion of Culture on the Plains*. Proceedings of the Fifteenth International Congress of Americanists.

———. 1914. The Influence of the Horse in the Development of Plains Culture. *American Anthropologist* 16:1–25.

———. 1917. *The American Indian*. New York: McMurtrie.

———. 1922. *North American Indians of the Plains*. New York: American Museum of Natural History.

———. 1926. *The Relation of Man to Nature in Aboriginal North America*. New York: D. Appleton-Century Co.

Wood, W. Raymond. 1980. Plains Trade in Prehistoric and Protohistoric Intertribal Relations. In *Anthropology on the Great Plains*, edited by W. Raymond Wood and Margot Liberty. Lincoln: University of Nebraska Press.

Wood, W. Raymond and Margot Liberty, editors. 1980. *Anthropology on the Great Plains*. Lincoln: University of Nebraska Press.

Some of the more prominent texts in this tradition include: Wissler 1906, 1914, 1917, 1922; Lowie 1916, 1927, 1954; Spier 1921; Webb 1932; Strong 1933; Smith 1938; Mishkin 1940; Secoy 1953; Ewers 1955; Roe 1955; Eggan 1966; and Wood and Liberty 1980.

The development and use of the culture area concept in respect to Native North America and the Plains in particular can be traced through the following texts: Mason 1896; Holmes 1903; Farrand 1904; Wissler 1917, 1926; Benedict 1932; Kroeber 1939; Driver 1961; Wilson 1963; Eggan 1966; Murdock 1967; and Driver and Coffin 1975. In addition, a regional plan of organization has been used in nearly every survey textbook of Native North America and is the primary organizing principle in the ongoing Smithsonian Handbook of North American Indians series.

The most prominent exponent of this view has since become John Ewers (1955) based on his study of Blackfoot trade with Euroamericans on the northern Plains. See also Albers and James 1986 and 1991.

Movies and other forms of popular representation have had similar difficulty in establishing continuity between the Indian past and the Indian present. *Cheyenne Autumn*, a film made by John Ford in 1964, depicted the end of prereservation Plains life by portraying the disappearance of the bison and the destitution of Cheyenne people. Thus, the movie draws a poignant close to ecological and economic ideas of the Plains and leaves us with a once proud people who are lost without the formative conditions of the region to shape and support their lives. Scholars have used the somewhat less melodramatic concept of acculturation to measure their same perception of the disappearance of "traditional" ways of life among Native peoples in the twentieth century.

Some discussion has also focused on intertribal trade for specialized food items (agricultural goods from villagers and meat from nomadic hunters). These efforts have, in essence, been attempts to assert the dominance of ecological explanations over economic explanations and have not been true attempts to articulate an integrated account of both ecological and economic constraints on Native organization and decision-making.

Some Plains archaeologists (Blakeslee 1975; Wood 1980; Vehik 1988) do have an interest in prehistoric exchange. That pre-contact trade, however, is treated as an adjunct to subsistence activities rather than as a primary economic activity (which is how Jablow characterizes Cheyenne trading activities in the historic period).

See my introduction to Mishkin's monograph for a fuller treatment of this alternative moment in Plains discourse (Foster 1992).

Certainly, personnel did shift among extrafamilial social units on the Plains, sometimes involving changes in ethnic or cultural identities. My point, though, is that these individual or family shifts did not fundamentally alter the relationships among those units and identities that constituted them as communities. Thus, some Plains Apaches joined Arapaho bands in the mid-nineteenth century but this did not result in any fundamental changes in the organization of either the Plains Apache or Arapaho communities. Albers also tends to take evidences of short-term co-residence or alliance as examples of merger. Instead, these are better interpreted as instances of mutually beneficial cooperation that did not have

long-term consequences for the different cultural communities of the participants.

Albers' treatment of Plains Apaches is a good example here. The Plains
Apaches are known in the scholarly literature as Kiowa-Apaches because they
were allied with Kiowas at different times in the nineteenth century. However,
Plains Apaches also were allied with Cheyennes, Comanches, and Arapahos during the same period. Albers assumes, based on secondary texts, that Plains
Apaches merged with Kiowas. Even the most cursory reading of primary texts,
though, makes clear that Plains Apaches treated these alliances as politically
and economically utilitarian while carefully maintaining their own separate language, religious beliefs and practices, social units, and community gatherings.
Had Albers undertaken anything more than a superficial reading of scholarly
texts about the southern Plains, she would have encountered these more dispersed statements about Plains Apache social and cultural organization.

PREFACE

The present study aims to examine economic relationships among the American Indian tribes of the Great Plains of the United States and southern Canada. The first end in view is to define the structure and function of intertribal trade among these groups. This must, perforce, be done against the background of the influence of the horse and the fur trade which, before the final conquest of the Indians, were the two most powerful factors affecting the aboriginal cultures. It will, thus, be necessary to view the Indian groups as functioning members of the White trade situation in which they were involved, and which was ultimately one of the most important influences on the trade activities maintained by the various tribes among themselves. Furthermore, it is essential also to evaluate the significance of the horse, not only as an object of trade, but also as an instrument of production which expanded trade. Since the horse and the fur trade were interacting and interdependent phenomena, they will be treated conjointly in their influence upon the aboriginal trade picture.

The study also explores the role of one tribal group in the complex of intertribal trade activities in relation to the role of other tribes and shows how these roles were affected by changing historical circumstances. And it further shows that an understanding of the dynamic influences of intertribal trade clarifies the nature of the relations between tribes within a culture area, such as that of the Plains, through observation of the manner in which a complex of tribal entities is subject to positive and negative forces with regard to each other under a specified set of conditions.

In addition, the study shows how further insight into the interrelationships of aspects of culture can be gained from the viewpoint of trade, and indicates how the influences of trade may provide a focus for viewing and, at least partially, explaining intra-tribal changes of various kinds. It is suggested that these may go so far as to involve a change in basic subsistence patterns. In this connection, it should be stated that although Plains political and warfare patterns have received considerable attention previously and are essential in a consideration of intertribal relations, they are here subordinated to the economic factors of trade.

Emphasis has been placed upon the Cheyenne Indians in this study essentially because the writer is more familiar with the data on that tribe. There is also another reason for selecting the Cheyenne as the focus of our interest in the present discussion. In the literature on the Indians of the Plains, attention has been directed to a shift, during historic times, in basic subsistence from horticulture to complete equestrian nomadism and semi-nomadism on the part of some tribes. Such tribes as the Arikara, Mandan, Hidatsa, and Pawnee, were originally fully sedentary, village-dwelling, horticultural people who later developed an increasing reliance upon the horse and a corresponding attenuation of some of their sedentary habits and aspects of their culture.[1] Continuing to employ their villages as permanent habitations and growing corn as a food staple, they also went out on buffalo hunts during part of the year. In the case of the Upper Missouri tribes such as the Mandan, Hidatsa, and Arikara, the fact that their villages also became trade centers militated against any very significant progression in the direction of nomadism. The Pawnee, on the other hand, went so far in developing equestrian buffalo hunting patterns that they hung themselves on the horns of a dilemma, so to speak. They did not make a complete nomadic adjustment, while at the same time their horticultural existence, which offered such rich social and ceremonial rewards, became so debilitated that they had no cultural stamina to resist either their Indian or White enemies.[2]

On the other hand, there were individual tribes, of which the Cheyenne are a classic example, that migrated from the northeastern periphery of the Great Plains, where they were sedentary horticulturalists, into the heart of the Plains to become so-called "typical" equestrian nomadic hunters.[3] Because the historical literature on them is subject to interpretation from the vantage point of intertribal trade, and because they exemplify so strikingly the aforementioned transition in basic subsistence, the Cheyenne may be regarded as a key group upon which certain historical factors such as the introduction of the horse and the fur trade exerted their combined influence.

In the process of adopting a new type of subsistence economy on the Plains, the Cheyenne at the same time assumed the role of middleman traders. Conducive to the assumption of this role was the fact of their new geographical location between the sources of supply of important exchangeable commodities – European manufactures entering the area via the Upper Missouri villages and horses coming into the Plains from the Southwest. In this situation, the Cheyenne facilitated the transmission of horses to the northeastern periphery of the Plains and brought in exchange European goods from the trade centers of the sedentary village tribes to the mobile hunters of the interior Plains. It is, therefore,

---

[1] This change is strikingly demonstrated on the archaeological level, especially in the case of the Pawnee. See Strong, 1935, p. 297.

[2] Ibid., pp. 297—299. See also Lesser, 1933.

[3] Similar migrations involving changes in basic subsistence patterns were made by tribes from culture areas adjacent to the Plains, e.g., bands of Cree and Ojibwa from the Woodlands, and the Coeur d'Alene from the Plateau.

suggested that the interpretation of the data presented in this study throws light on the dynamics of the change from horticulture to equestrian nomadism, which up to now has not been satisfactorily demonstrated.

Until the first quarter of the nineteenth century the contacts of the Cheyenne with travelers, explorers, or fur traders were never extensive. The few individuals who did spend any appreciable length of time in their midst were illiterate traders or employes of traders who left no records except casual references to their sojourn among them.[4] Nevertheless, there is a body of literature, recorded by men who had varying amounts of contact with the Cheyenne and the tribes with whom that group had intercourse, containing considerable information relevant to the subject of our discussion. The period with which we are chiefly concerned extends from about 1795 until approximately 1840, a span of time containing documentation most useful for purposes of the problem considered here in that it provides a dynamic panorama of intertribal trade relations up to the beginning of the breakdown of that trade under pressure of the "westward march of empire."

I am grateful to Professor W. D. Strong not only for introducing me to the Cheyenne via the route of archaeology, but also for helpful guidance and encouragement in exploring the possibilities of the material on that tribe. I wish to thank Professor Julian H. Steward and Dr. Gene Weltfish for trenchant criticisms and suggestions for improving various sections of this study. I cannot do less than express my deep appreciation to Dr. Alexander Lesser, whose brief contact with the materials of this study provided me with new and illuminating insights concerning its implications. I am especially indebted to Dr. Marian W. Smith for giving unselfishly and unstintingly of her time, effort and knowledge of the Plains Indian in long and fruitful discussions which immeasurably enhanced the final product. Profound thanks are also due her for invaluable aid in the preparation of the manuscript.

I cannot conclude these remarks without acknowledging my everlasting gratitude to my wife, Alta Gusar Jablow. There is little doubt in my mind that without her constant encouragement and stimulation, without her patient help in ways too numerous to mention, this study could not have been accomplished.

November, 1950,   Joseph Jablow
Brooklyn College, New York.

---

[4] Nasatir, 1927. Appended to this article (pp. 57—71) are documents on the Spanish exploration of the Upper Missouri, translated and edited by Nasatir, including depositions made by men who had been with the Cheyenne in the Upper Missouri area in 1794.

TABLE OF CONTENTS

MAPS

CHAPTER ONE

DYNAMIC HISTORICAL INFLUENCES ON THE PLAINS

Some Aspects of Cheyenne History

Although the Cheyenne, within a period of approximately three hundred years, experienced four modes of life involving three distinct transitions, their activities as traders encompass a relatively short time span. If they participated in the developing trade of the northeastern forest tribes of North America during the sixteenth and seventeenth centuries before their advent onto the Plains, history has failed to record that fact. Material on Cheyenne trade does not appear until after the middle of the eighteenth century, during the period of their transition to a Plains type of existence.

The nature of the traditional material makes it reasonable to assume that preceding their advent into Minnesota they had a type of economy in which the hunting of small game was predominant.[1] This was followed by a semi-sedentary horticultural period of earth-lodge dwelling until at least the third quarter of the eighteenth century when they were in the process of assuming their third type of existence based on equestrian buffalo hunting and trading in the Great Plains. The latter was the hey-day of the Cheyenne people during which this pattern was continued until the end of the Indian wars in the latter part of the nineteenth century. There followed immediately the fourth, the final, the inglorious phase of reservation life which was not adopted without a last burst of defiance in the name of human dignity and decency.

The early history of the Cheyenne has been dealt with by Mooney,[2] Dorsey,[3] Will,[4] Clark,[5] and especially by Grinnell[6] whose various works on that group make one of the finest tributes ever accorded the American aborigine. The purpose of this chapter is, therefore, not merely to summarize generally the information provided by the foregoing authors. It attempts to re-evaluate certain historical data with regard to their effect upon the Cheyenne and to incorporate into the total picture the recently acquired archaeological information on that tribe.[6a]

---

[1] Grinnell, 1923b, Vol. I, pp. 5 and 51; Grinnell, 1926, pp. 244—245; Dorsey, 1905, Vol. IX, No. 1, p. 34; Will, 1914, p. 68.

[2] Mooney, 1905—07; also his article on the Cheyenne in Hodge, 1907.

[3] Dorsey, 1905.   [4] Will, 1914.   [5] Clark, 1885, pp. 99ff.

[6] Grinnell, 1915, 1923b, 1926, and numerous articles.

[6a] Columbia University-North Dakota Historical Society Expedition, 1938.

1

In tracing their movements from the northeast into the Great Plains both documented history and native traditions have been relied upon. As regards native sources, for present purposes it is sufficient to indicate that the migration legends and traditions of the Cheyenne clearly point to a Central Algonkian provenience, probably on the Canadian side of the Great Lakes.[7] This evidence is supported by the fact that when the first casual references are made to them by the early French explorers, traders and cartographers, they are located in south central Minnesota. In addition, there are Dakota traditions to the effect that the Cheyenne were already living in the Minnesota River valley when the former first came there.[8] On the whole, they seem to have been a small Algonkian-speaking group whose destiny became linked more closely, during the latter part of the seventeenth and early eighteenth centuries, with their Siouan neighbors than with their linguistic and early cultural congeners.

Since oral traditions are primarily useful in denoting general trends and directions in the past life of a people, we shall begin our inquiry with a consideration of the factual data contained in European historical records. The first reference to the Cheyenne appears on a map of Joliet and Franquelin which, according to Neill, was apparently made before 1673.[9] They are here called "Chaiena" and are listed together with seven other tribes on the east side of the Mississippi River some distance above the Wisconsin. The "Siou" are also shown on the same side below this group of tribal names. In the third quarter of the seventeenth century the Cheyenne are, therefore, placed in western Wisconsin, just over the border of southeastern Minnesota.

On the 24th of February, 1680, while La Salle was building Fort Crevecoeur near the present site of Peoria, Illinois, he was visited by a group named Chaa who asked him to come to their home at the head of the great river, where, they said, they had a large number of beaver and other furs.[10] Although their claimed habitat certainly coincided with all the evidence for their known location at that period, attention must be called to the fact that the Cheyenne word for themselves is *tsĭs tsĭs' tăs*. The term by which they have come to be known is derived from a Sioux word *shā hĭ' yē na*, connoting those who speak an unintelligible language.[11] Unfortunately, La Salle does not state by whom they were called Chaa. Nevertheless, those who have considered the evidence seem to be agreed that it was very likely the Cheyenne whom La Salle saw 300 or more air-line miles from their home on the Upper Mississippi.[12]

[7] Mooney, 1905—07, p. 363; Grinnell, 1923, Vol. 1, pp. 4, 6, and 16, and 1926, pp. XIV and XV; Will, 1914, p. 68.

[8] Hyde, 1937, p. 9; Williamson, 1872, p. 296; Comfort, 1873, p. 402.

[9] Neill, 1883, p. 797.   [10] Margry, 1879, Vol. II, p. 54.

[11] Grinnell, 1923b, Vol. I, p. 2; Riggs, 1893, p. 193.

[12] Will, 1914, p. 67; Grinnell, 1923b, Vol. I, pp. 3 and 15; Mooney, 1905—07, and Hodge, 1907, Part I, p. 251.

According to Will, "Franquelin's map of 1688 places the Cheyenne on the Minnesota River," while another of his maps, approximately twelve years later, in about 1700 locates them on the Sheyenne River in North Dakota.[13] Although this is east of the point on the river where the only known Cheyenne horticultural village site has been located and excavated,[14] it does tie in with the later historical references to that village which quite definitely place it on the Sheyenne.[15] Traditionally, the Cheyenne are said to have lived in a village on the Minnesota River above the Otoes, while the Iowa were situated below the latter.[16] When Le Sueur, in October of 1700, founded his post at the mouth of the Blue Earth River on his journey up the Minnesota, he met "nine Scioux, who told him that the river belonged to the Scioux of the West, the Ayavois (Iowa), and Otoctatas (Oto), who lived a little farther off,..."[17] The fact that the Cheyenne are not mentioned in this connection, when taken together with the information provided by Franquelin's map of 1688, would seem to bear out the inference that they had probably moved up the Minnesota to Big Stone Lake and Lake Traverse,[18] and thence up the Red River from which they branched off at the Sheyenne where Franquelin's later map places them by 1700.

From what we know of the warlike ardor of the (Dakota) Sioux tribes, which (during the latter part of the seventeenth and early eighteenth centuries) were beyond question in a dominant position over most of Minnesota, it seems entirely plausible that the Cheyenne considered it expedient to withdraw from their territory to avoid continued depredations, if not by the Sioux, then at the hands of the latter's enemies. From the time the Pottowatomie were met in flight from the Dakotas at Soult St. Marie in 1641 by Joques and Raymbault,[19] the latter tribes are recorded as being continually embroiled with one or another of their enemies at various times. Until about 1666 they are mentioned in conflict with the Huron and Ottawa,[20] who were driven westward by the Iroquois, and also with the Ojibwa, with whom their constant wars were only occasionally interrupted by relatively short periods of peace. In 1669, Father Marquette wrote, "the Nadouessi are the Iroquois of this country...;" and again "all the lake tribes make war on them, but with small success."[21]

[13] Will, 1914, p. 69.
[14] Strong, 1940, particularly the section on the Sheyenne-Cheyenne site, pp. 370—376.
[15] See below, discussion on Sheyenne-Cheyenne site; and Strong, 1940, pp. 370—371.
[16] Will, 1914, p. 69; Mooney, 1905—07, p. 364; Hyde, 1937, p. 9; Riggs, 1893, p. 194; Williamson, 1880, pp. 283—284; Williamson, 1872, p. 296.
[17] Neill, 1883, p. 162.
[18] Will, 1914, p. 68; Riggs, 1893, p. 194; Grinnell, 1923b, Vol. I, pp. 16—17.
[19] Neill, 1883, p. 101.   [20] *Ibid.*, pp. 103—110.   [21] *Ibid.*, p. 111.

After having become embroiled with the Dakotas in the winter of
1670, the Huron and Ojibwa, who had been settled around the Jesuit
mission at Bayfield, Wisconsin, decided to leave the area in the following spring rather than risk hostilities with a league of Siouan tribes.
After the mission had been abandoned, the Dakotas, in 1674, became
involved in warfare with the Cree.[22] In September of 1679, Du Luth
successfully made peace between the Assiniboin and some other tribes,
and the Dakotas.[23] In April of 1680, Hennepin met thirty-three canoes of
a Dakota war party moving against the Illinois and Miami.[24] In 1685,
the Dakotas were temporarily allied with the Ojibwa in a war with the
Miami, Mascoutin and Foxes.[25] Between 1689 and 1695, "The Fox,
Mascoutin and others disturbed the traders, as well as the missionaries,
not only by their inter-tribal warfare, but also by the objections to
French trade and work with the Dakota and other tribes to the west."[26]
Furthermore, according to the questionable information provided by
La Hontan, the Dakotas were also under attack by the Iroquois during
this period.[27]

While on his way up the Mississippi River in July, 1700, beyond the
mouth of the Illinois, Le Sueur received a letter from Father Marest of
the Mission Immaculate Conception of the Holy Virgin, in Illinois, which
stated that "the Saugiestas have been defeated by the Scioux and
Ayavois (Iowa). The people have formed an alliance with the Quin-
capous (Kickapoos), some of the Mecoutins (Mascoutin), Renards
(Fox), and Metesigamias, and gone to revenge themselves, not on the
Scious, for they are too much afraid of them, but perhaps on the
Ayavois, or very likely upon the Paoutees(?), or more probably upon
the Osages, for these suspect nothing, and the others are on their
guard."[28] As we have seen above, a few months later, in October of the
same year, when Le Sueur reached the mouth of the Blue Earth in his
passage up the Minnesota River, he was told by the Sioux that the river
belonged to the Sioux of the West, the Iowa and Oto. But when, towards the end of the month, two Canadians left the newly completed
Fort L'Huillier to find the Iowa and Oto and invite them to settle in
its vicinity for purposes of providing agricultural produce and labor for
the mines which Le Sueur hoped to work, they could not locate the two
tribes.[29] By the middle of November, information was received, apparently from the Sioux, that the Iowa and Oto had left for the Missouri
River region to settle in the vicinity of the Omaha.[30]

[22] *Ibid.*, pp. 112—113.   [23] *Ibid.*, p. 122.
[24] *Ibid.*, p. 128.   [25] *Ibid.*, pp. 138—139.
[26] Mekeel, 1943, p. 149.   [27] *Ibid.*
[28] Neill, 1883, pp. 154—155. Saugiestas may refer to the Sauk or the Saulteurs
(Chippewa); see Hodge, 1907, p. 471. I have found no identification for the
Metesigamias.
[29] *Ibid.*, p. 165.   [30] *Ibid.*, p. 166.

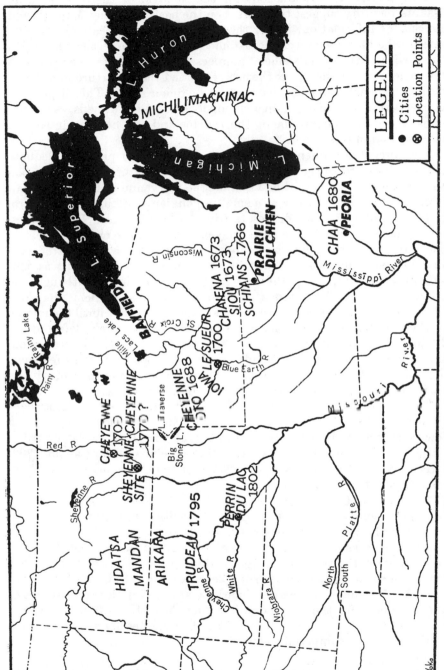

Map 1. Early Locations of the Cheyenne and Related Tribes.

Two alternative explanations for the removal of these tribes from Dakota territory suggest themselves on the basis of Father Marest's and Le Sueur's information. Either they left to avoid reprisals by the enemies of the Sioux who were accustomed to wreak their vengeance upon the weaker of the latter's allies – a process that must have been going on for some time; or the Sioux themselves forced the departure in order to derive the benefits of exclusive trade at Le Sueur's post. This disposition on the part of a tribe to retain a monopoly on a trader's goods, especially guns, was quite general among the Indians and will be considered in a later section of this paper.

The foregoing sequence of events would seem to provide adequate clues with regard to the nature of the external pressures operating upon the Cheyenne. We may thus visualize the Cheyenne in the second half of the seventeenth century as a small Algonkian-speaking, horticultural group, neighbors on the Minnesota River of horticultural Siouan tribes, all of whom, especially the alien Cheyenne, were more or less subject to the activities of the relatively mobile hunting Dakotas. The latter were involved with numerous other tribes in wars whose character was considerably intensified by the introduction of firearms. Although the advantage obviously rested with those who possessed them, the Cree, Chippewa, and tribes east of the Great Lakes, it was not until the middle of the eighteenth century that the Chippewa so decisively defeated the Dakotas that the latter were forced to retire from the Mille Lacs region. Even up to that time, the Dakotas apparently possessed very few guns and resisted their enemies, especially in the seventeenth century, by their numbers, military prowess, and the bow and arrow.[31]

The Cheyenne undoubtedly felt the reverberations of the almost continuous warfare of the Sioux, and were apparently affected by them a few years before the Iowa and Oto. For at the time the latter tribes withdrew from the Minnesota River, Franquelin's map of about 1700, already referred to, indicates the village of the Cheyenne on the Sheyenne River of North Dakota.

The struggle between the tribes in the Dakota region was, of course, not only a manifestation of aboriginal hostilities, but also included the effects of the rivalry of the British and French for a rich, fur-bearing colonial prize, as has so often been pointed out. In this struggle for territorial control, the two powers used various tribes as pawns to carry out their designs, arming their Indian allies against the Indians of the other side. But inasmuch as we are primarily concerned with the activities of the aborigines for the purpose of inferring their effects upon the Cheyenne and their movements, we need not be detained by a consideration of the question of imperial rivalries.[32]

[31] Mekeel, 1943, p. 151.
[32] On this subject see Mekeel, 1943. Also Mooney, 1905—07, pp. 364—365.

It is not until well over a half century later that we find the Cheyenne again mentioned in the historical literature, when they are referred to by Carver in 1766 as one of the eight bands of the Sioux of the Plains.[33] Unfortunately, he did not visit all these groups and only wintered with a large party of Sioux "whose language I perfectly acquired during a residence of seven months," which by his own dates (December 1766 through April 1767) turns out to have been only five months.[34] Had he actually met the Cheyenne he could not have failed to become aware of the fact that his "perfect" knowledge of the Dakota tongue was less than useless among them. However, this direct association of the Cheyenne with the western bands of the Dakotas may provide a possible clue to the transition of at least some groups of the former to a buffalo hunting economy. The point is of particular interest in this connection because we have evidence which seems to indicate that just at about this time the Cheyenne village on Sheyenne River was either still inhabited by members of the tribe who were engaged in horticultural pursuits, or that the settlement had only recently been destroyed. It is not possible to fix accurately the date of occupancy of this site. But it seems safe to say, as other writers have suggested, that between 1700 and about 1770 the Cheyenne were undergoing a process of change which eventuated in their becoming complete equestrian nomads by the end of the eighteenth century.[35]

According to Will, "while located on the Sheyenne River the Cheyenne entered upon their life on the real plains, and here their transition into a plains tribe began."[36] Grinnell conceives the process somewhat more dynamically when he says, "it is probable that at the time when some of the villages were permanently situated at certain points, a part of the Cheyenne were still pushing westward, and that the tribe was partly migratory and partly sedentary, some established at one place and some moving about. It is possible that the permanent villages ... in Minnesota and on the Sheyenne River ..., and perhaps others, were occupied during the same period, ... and that other groups may then have been wandering about on the plains after the buffalo."[37]

There were other Cheyenne villages on the Missouri which may have been settled either while the Sheyenne River site was a going concern or shortly thereafter.[38] But the fact, nevertheless, remains that the Cheyenne who were met by Trudeau when he was among the Arikara in 1795

[33] Carver, 1778, pp. 79—80.
[34] *Ibid.*, p. 76.
[35] See below, discussion of Sheyenne-Cheyenne site.
[36] Will, 1914, pp. 69—70.
[37] Grinnell, 1923b, Vol. I, pp. 14—15.
[38] Will, 1914, p. 76; Lewis and Clark, in Thwaites, 1904, Vol. I, p. 195; Grinnell, 1923b, Vol. I, p. 16. See also Grinnell, 1923b, pp. 23—29, and 1918, pp. 359—380.

were a fully developed equestrian buffalo hunting group.[39] This would obviously imply that certain bands had become such some years ago, while horticulture was still being practiced by other groups. Even as late as 1802, Perrin Du Lac states that the Cheyenne, whom he met at the White River on the Missouri, still planted maize and tobacco although they were nomadic hunters during most of the year.[40]

Although, as has been stated, the date of abandonment of the Sheyenne River site is problematical, there are certain clues in the literature as to its general period. John Hay, in his notes on McKay's and Evans' Journals, which together cover the period 1787—1797, tells of his own journey into the Northwest made in 1794. He refers to the fact that the Cheyenne formerly resided on the Sheyenne branch of the Red River and claims the Cheyenne were forced to leave that village and go to the Missouri because of the Assiniboin and Sioux, but he does not state when this might have occurred.[41] David Thompson, however, writing in 1799, gives a detailed account of the destruction of what is *presumably* the Sheyenne River village, though location and time are not specifically mentioned.[42] This was told him by the Chippewa chief who led the attacking party of about one hundred and fifty men, and is of special interest because archaeological evidence bears out the statements made by the chief in two crucial instances. In the first place, the Chippewa states not only that there were horses in the village, but also that the majority of the occupants had just gone out hunting on horses. This information is corroborated by the finding of horse bones associated with contemporaneous material.[43] Secondly, the chief said that the party "quickly set fire to the village." The abundance of charred and burned timbers in the lodges excavated are ample testimony to the truth of what actually happened. Although this coincidence of facts from two separate sources can by no means be considered proof positive, it would appear to lend weight to the inference that we are here dealing with the Sheyenne-Cheyenne site. Among the few captives taken by the Chippewas to their camp on Rainy River was an infant who was sent to Rainy River House where he was brought up. Swanton has suggested that if the dates of the Rainy River House could be determined it might be

[39] Trudeau, 1914, pp. 453 ff.

[40] Perrin Du Lac, 1807, p. 63.

[41] Quaife, 1916, p. 208. Lewis and Clark, a few years later, make an almost identical statement when they write that the Cheyenne "formerly resided on a branch of the Red River of Lake Winnipie, which still bears their name. Being oppressed by the Sioux, they removed to the west side of the Missouri..." (Thwaites, 1904, Vol. VI, p. 100).

[42] Thompson in Tyrrell, 1916, pp. 261—263. John R. Swanton first called attention to this account and commented on it in an article, (1930, pp. 156—160).

[43] Strong, 1940, p. 373.

possible to date the destruction of the village, but adds it is unlikely it could have been much before 1790.[44] This surmise is probably based on the fact that the North West Company, which had a fort on Rainy River within a mile of Rainy Lake, was not organized until the winter of 1783—1784,[45] while the Hudson's Bay Company built its first establishment in the same vicinity in 1793.[46] The only other possibility is that a Rainy River House might have been built earlier by one of the trading interests which eventually became a part of the North west Company, though there does not seem to be any direct evidence for this supposition. Ezra Stiles' extract of Peter Pond's map of his travels between 1773 and 1790 shows an establishment "No. 2" on the Canadian side of Rainy River above Rainy Lake, but there is no date for it, and so it still could have been built after 1784.[47]

Alexander Henry, the younger, writing in 1800, lends credence to Thompson's story that the Sheyenne River village was destroyed by the Chippewas, but on the other hand, states that the event took place in about 1740.[48] Inasmuch as the appearance of horses in the region of the Upper Missouri tribes is first mentioned in 1738 and 1739 by the Verendryes,[49] and the latter actually obtained horses in the same vicinity during the winter of 1742—43, the destruction of the Sheyenne village undoubtedly occurred some time after those dates, since the Cheyenne apparently had already sufficient horses to cause the Chippewas to fear encountering "Cavalry in the Plains."[50]

A further clue toward the dating of this site is provided in Haines' analysis of the diffusion of the horse in the Plains area, where he states that ". . . Carver found a few horses at Prairie du Chien in 1766, but the Sioux whom he met in central Minnesota that same year were using canoes rather than horses. . . Peter Pond, trading in the same area six years later, found horses in common use among the Sioux who, he says, are the same ones visited by Carver. David Thompson, writing in 1796, reported that the Sioux were then using horses instead of canoes, indicating that they had made the change in comparatively recent times or it would not have been worth the emphasis he gave it."[51]

[44] Swanton, 1930, p. 159.   [45] Davidson, 1918, pp. 9—12.
[46] Nute, 1941 b, pp. 42—43. See also Nute, 1941 a, p. 270.
[47] Davidson, 1918, pp. 42—43.
[48] Coues, 1897, Vol. 1, pp. 144—145.
[49] Verendrye, 1914, p. 351. On the basis of the Verendrye Journals "covering the period 1735—1743, it is clear that there were no horses north and east of the Missouri River in the Dakotas until one of the sons brought two of the animals from the vicinity of the Black Hills to the Canadian posts. Horses had as yet appeared only occasionally on the southern bank of the Missouri opposite the Mandan villages. The real limit of horse using Indians was the Black Hills country, the Mandans having acquired no horses yet although they had been trading with horse Indians for several years," (Haines, 1938, p. 433).
[50] Tyrrell, 1916, p. 262.   [51] Haines, 1938, p. 434.

Thus, horses became common among the Sioux between 1766 and 1772. In this connection, it is well to refer to an oft-quoted Cheyenne tradition to the effect that some time after they had penetrated the Missouri River region on to the Black Hills, the Sioux began coming in. "They declared that the first Sioux who came were very poor and had no horses, which the Cheyennes had already obtained...; that when the Sioux came, carrying their possessions on dog travois, the Cheyenne took pity on them and occasionally gave them a horse; that this generosity resulted in the coming of more and more Sioux to receive like presents,..."[52] As we have seen previously, the Cheyenne did move westward in advance of the Sioux. This tradition, then, would appear to strengthen the probability that at least some bands of Cheyenne already had the horse by the time that animal became common among the Sioux. While we could thus say that some Cheyenne got horses between 1742 and 1770, it actually puts us no nearer a precise dating of the Sheyenne River village. Although Strong's estimate of 1770 is probably nearly correct, the question still remains open.[53]

If it is not possible to determine the exact nature of the process of change undergone by the Cheyenne from a horticultural existence, we nevertheless have the evidence of Trudeau, who engaged in direct trade with them, that by 1794 – 95 they were fully developed equestrian nomad hunters.[54] From this time on they are mentioned only as such in the literature, with the exception of Perrin Du Lac, 1802, to whom reference has already been made. Tabeau's account, covering the period 1803—1805, shows clearly that the Cheyenne, far from planting, were trading products of the hunt with the Arikara for agricultural produce.[55] Grinnell's old informants, however, stated that up until the middle of the nineteenth century and thereafter, individual women "commonly planted corn patches as their mothers before them had done, and had taught them to do."[56] Such statements obviously do not vitiate the basic fact of the later orientation of the Cheyenne subsistence pattern around buffalo hunting. And it is as equestrian nomads that the Cheyenne are important for the purpose of the present study.

The External Historical Forces

Prior to the subjugation of the Plains Indians by force of arms and their subsequent settlement on reservations, the two outstanding events which produced major changes in their lives were the introduction of the horse and the introduction of European goods through the fur trade. For the most part, the influence of each of these factors has been considered

[52] Grinnell, 1915, p. 34. See also Will, 1914, p. 77; and Hyde, 1937, pp. 20—21.
[53] Strong, 1940, p. 371.   [54] Trudeau, 1914, pp. 453 ff.
[55] Abel, 1939, p. 152.   [56] Grinnell, 1923 b, Vol. I, p. 253.

separately. The earliest study, by Wissler,[57] conceived the influence of the horse in terms of an intensification and diffusion of cultural traits already in existence at the time of the advent of that animal. Mishkin's more recent interpretation emphasizes the important problem of qualitative change in the socio-economic structure of the tribes which incorporated the horse into their way of life.[58] Lewis' study of the Blackfoot, on the other hand, has shown the effects of White contact in the form of the fur trade on some of the social institutions of that group.[59] Although the interpretations made in these studies have emphasized one or the other of the two historical factors alluded to, they have all recognized that both were important in effecting change. For purposes of analysis and elucidation they have been treated as separate phenomena, whereas from the point of view of intertribal trade relations they are in reality interacting and inter-dependent. Almost thirty-five years ago Wissler, in a sense, already recognized this when he wrote,

> ... the possession of this new means of transportation (the horse) and this new element of property would no doubt act as a cultural stimulant... We must not, however, too hastily conclude that the introduction of the horse during the seventeenth century was the chief cause of this. The presence of the white traders on the continent must be considered. Firearms were soon in the hands of the tribes ... then again the trade by which they were received created new demands, new wants, and so stimulated production...[60]

In order to see the problem clearly in terms of the total perspective of the historical situation, the significance of the horse must be regarded in its relation to the fur trade which was supplying a constant stream of material goods. These products of European manufacture the Indian came to rely upon, and his activity as a producer for the European market assumed larger proportions than it did for the native market. Although the horse was of fundamental importance in the tribal economy for procuring buffalo, and for meeting the aesthetic or psychological needs of the people, the intensity of activity surrounding the horse would hardly have been as great without the stimulus of the White trade which not only created native needs requiring satisfaction, but also had its own need for horses. With the passage of time and the expansion of the American frontier farther westward, involving migrations of hundreds of thousands of Whites from the east, the market for horses expanded enormously.

But from the Indian point of view, the horse was important primarily because it made life easier – in hunting, riding, and in the capacity of a beast of burden. Whatever delights and attractions European articles offered, his living still had to be made by the employment of the horse as an instrument of production for food, clothing and shelter. Beyond the

[57] Wissler, 1914.
[58] Mishkin, 1940.
[59] Lewis, 1942.
[60] Wissler, 1914, p. 15.

satisfaction of his primary subsistence requirements by means of the hunt, he was able to produce and transport a surplus which was used in trade with other tribes.

In their activities as traders Indians were actually engaged in two economic systems which interpenetrated in various ways. On the one hand they functioned in a system of intertribal trade, while on the other, they were producers and traders in furs in the European mercantile system. Although similar types of goods were produced for, and exchanged in, both systems by the Indians, the emphases varied in each. Given the stimulus provided by the introduction of European commodities the Indians became producers for a European market in which they traded directly with Whites from whom they acquired European goods; or they traded for those goods with other Indians who had themselves secured them from European traders. In the last analysis, it was the production of furs by the Indians which brought them European commodities for exchange. But once these goods had been introduced into the aboriginal trade system it became possible to exchange them for another highly desirable commodity – the horse. In fact, in the interior of the Great Plains the horse was the medium of exchange for securing guns and other objects of European manufacture. As a result, there was a constant stimulus for the acquisition of horses to be used in trade. In addition, there was a considerable surplus production of food, skins, clothes and ornaments which played an important part in intertribal exchanges, while European traders operating in the field were to a large degree dependent for their subsistence upon food produced by the Indians. On this level the horse again was important as an instrument of production for equestrian buffalo hunters. It is, therefore, apparent that in the total trade situation the Indian was a producer and trader in both the native and European market.

Effect of the Horse on Trade Relations

In his description of the Salishan tribes of the Plateau, Teit shows clearly how in many respects the character of intertribal trade was affected by the introduction of the horse. Tribes which were formerly dependent upon trade for the procurement of certain articles were, by means of the horse, enabled to produce those objects themselves. Thus, "Before the advent of the horse, a good many buffalo robes were bought from the Pend d'Oreilles and Flathead..." by the Coeur d'Alene, whereas afterwards they were no longer dependent upon others for this article except for the especially good ones they got from the Plains tribes. They supplied the latter with fish products, which they traded from the groups farther west, with horses, bows and arrows, and luxury articles. In this particular instance, it was not a simple matter of the horse enabling the Coeur d'Alene to provide themselves with additional materials to make them independent producers. Mishkin[61] has already called attention to Teit's data which indicate that the horse effected an almost complete economic revolution among the Coeur d'Alene from which there followed, in turn, a change not only in the nature of the trade (the kind, quality, and quantity of goods) but also in the trade relations between specific groups. "An impetus was given to trading. While formerly trade was chiefly with the Western tribes, now much trading was also done with those to the east. Commodities were exchanged more rapidly, and came from greater distances."[62] Just as the horse "drew (the Coeur d'Alene) away from the lakes, and in great measure from fishing, canoes, bark, and wood, materials which they were accustomed to use..."[63] so it would appear to be justifiable to assume that the same animal, in addition to the circumstances described in the previous section, was an important factor in drawing the Cheyenne away from their previous horticultural existence on the northeastern periphery of the Plains.[64]

The nature of the exchange which took place between the Plains and Plateau in the expanded trade horizons stimulated by the horse is exemplified in the following passage:

> It seems that in olden times the Coeur d'Alene did nearly all their trading with the Spokan, and comparatively little with other tribes. After they began to go to the Plains a trade sprang up in special articles with several of the Plains tribes. All parties going to the plains to hunt buffalo carried small quantities of western products to trade, for the Plains tribes were very fond of some of these, and were willing to pay rather high prices. Thus salmon oil put up in sealed salmon skins, salmon pemmican mixed with oil and put up in salmon skins, cakes of camas and other roots, cakes of certain kinds of berries, Indian hemp and Indian hemp-twine were transported across the mountains...
> The Plains Indians also desired arrows and bows of horn and wood, which they considered better than their own; also shells, certain kinds of beads, necklaces peculiar to the west, and greenstone pipes. They were also anxious to buy western horses; and most parties drove a considerable number of spare horses along, partly as remounts, but most of them for sale. Skins and clothes were also traded and interchanged. In exchange feather bonnets of the best kind and buffalo robes of the finest sort were obtained. The best bonnets and robes of the Plains tribes were considered better than their own. The feather bonnets most desired were of the Sioux style. Some of them were made by the Crow. The buffalo robes desired were of the softest tan, and ornamented with a band of beadwork across the middle. The Crow robes were most highly valued. Often a horse and, in addition, a wellmade leather shirt, was paid for one of the best kinds of robes. Catlinite, and catlinite pipes were also often bought from the Plains tribes...[65]

[61] Mishkin, 1940, pp. 12—13.   [62] Teit, 1930, p. 152.   [63] *Ibid.*, p. 151.
[64] However, as will be suggested later, in the conclusions to this study, it was not the horse *per se* which exerted this influence, but the horse in a special context of historical circumstances.
[65] Teit, op. cit., pp. 113—114.

It should be noted here that apart from the fish and luxury items, like shells, necklaces, etc., the products forming part of the exchange were actually made in both areas: the Plains and the Plateau. What was important to the respective trading parties was the *quality* of the objects concerned; the differences in this respect being due partly to the differences in the nature of the materials found in each geographical area, and partly to differences in technique of manufacture. Thus, the Plains Indians got *better* bows, arrows and horses from the Coeur d'Alene, while the latter, in turn, received the *best* feather bonnets and ornamented buffalo robes. Before the advent of the horse this type of trade could hardly have existed to any significant extent.

For the fish products obtained from the people on the Thompson and Lower Fraser rivers, the Salishan people gave "...horses, dressed buffalo skins and robes, dressed moose skin (rarely caribou skin), painted buffalo hide bags and parfleches and woven bags of the Nez Perce type."[66]

It is apparent that with greater ease of communication and transport, the tempo of commodity exchange was not only accelerated, but the territory encompassed in the process was very significantly expanded. Furthermore, the number of people participating in trade increased as less time had to be consumed in meeting basic subsistence needs. The quantity of trade goods naturally increased, and their nature changed from luxuries to more useful objects.

It is important to note also that when the horse came into widespread use "the old trade routes became of minor importance. Trade now passed across country with the greatest ease. The new main trade routes followed across the rolling, lightly timbered grassy plateaus, and through open valleys, in almost straight lines from one place to another."[67] As these trade routes changed, the direction of flow of cultural influences connected with trade changed correspondingly, and different tribes were affected as a result.

Thus it seems that before the introduction of the horse the Shuswap and Thompson tribes were exposed to less influence through trade from the southeast and the plains and to more from the south and Oregon country. As the old trade routes led more directly to the Shuswap than to the Thompson, the former tribe would be more influenced by whatever cultural influences followed them. After the introduction of the horse, conditions were reversed; and these tribes came under a considerably greater influence from the southeast, which before long was further augmented by the great annual movements of the more eastern of the Plateau tribes to the plains for buffalo hunting. The trade routes which now came into vogue led rather to the Thompson than to the Shuswap, and therefore the former tribe now became subject to influences brought in by trade.[68]

[66] *Ibid.*, p. 253.   [67] *Ibid.*, p. 252.   [68] *Ibid.*, p. 253.

The Horse as a Commodity in Trade

Good horses were constantly in demand in the Plains tribal economy itself and had to be continually replenished, both for subsistence purposes in the hunt and for accumulation of goods to be used in trade. In the acquisition of European goods from tribes which had access to them, either directly or indirectly, horses were the favored medium of exchange. It can therefore be seen that a constant stream of these animals had to be kept flowing into the Plains area in order to meet the requirements of both hunting and trade. However, the trading for horses between Plateau and Plains referred to by Teit, was not by any means the predominant source of the animals for the Plains tribes, though it was the original avenue through which horses were introduced to the northern Plains, specifically to the Blackfoot and the Crow.[69] It was from the middle to the end of the eighteenth century that this route was of significance; but certainly the rest of the Plains groups did not receive their horses from the Plateau area in anywhere near the quantity they required. The stream of animals supplying the great majority of Plains tribes had its ultimate source in the Spanish southwest and Mexico, where the main raiding of the stock of the rancherias was done by such tribes as the Comanche, Kiowa, and Apache.[70] But it was the Comanche who were the greatest raiders of them all, and the Spanish documents of the latter part of the eighteenth century are replete with accounts of the depredations of those fearful nomads of the Southern Plains.[71]

The acquisition and movement of horses among the tribes may be visualized in terms of direct and indirect sources. The Spanish territory may be conceived of as the direct source of supply, and the importance of the Comanche as a source of horses for the rest of the Plains may be gleaned from such a passage as this:

> ... (the northern tribes of the Spanish territory in the southwest) all visit each other and they observe mutual friendship, although that of the Comanches is accustomed to alteration; but it is renewed in a short time, for, being impelled by necessity, they do not hesitate to sell the horses which the

[69] "When not at war, the Coeur d'Alene and western tribes in early times always sold horses to the Plains tribes, but no horses were procured by western tribes from eastern tribes" (*Ibid.*, p. 110). In addition, Haines, in his excellent study, writes that the Blackfoot, Crow, and other tribes first received their horses from the Shoshone of southern Idaho (1938, p. 436).

[70] As Mishkin has suggested "... in the case of the northern Plains the greater the distance from Texan and Mexican rancherias, the fewer horses found among the Indian tribes. The southwestern Plains and the western marginal peoples who raided toward the southwest were the richest, while those who were not in direct contact with the original source of horses had to raid neighboring Indian tribes..." Mishkin, 1940, p. 11. See also Richardson, 1933, p. 71; Mooney, 1898, p. 165.

[71] Bolton, 1914.

others lack on account of the frequent robberies which they experience from
the Apache and Osagues, and the loss of which they can supply only by the
trade of the Comanches.[72]

Horses with Spanish brands eventually found their way up into
Canada from tribe to tribe.[73]

The indirect source of supply was the Indian tribes themselves, who
raided from each other. This was obviously less tedious and time-consuming a method of obtaining horses than making the long journey to
Mexico or the Southwest through enemy territory and then risk losing
the herds on the return trip.[74] Apart from this factor of chance, there
were few who could afford to neglect their families and responsibilities.
Nevertheless, the Cheyenne, on occasion, did venture down into the
Spanish settlements,[75] but their chief reliance was on raiding from other
tribes such as the Pawnee, Comanche and the Kiowa,[76] and upon their
trade with the Arapaho, Comanche and Kiowa. The tribes with the
largest herds of horses, the Kiowa and the Comanche, were nearest the
direct source, and from them the horses, by processes of trading and
raiding found their way up to the Northern Plains.[77]

The Creation of New Needs by the Fur Trade

As the influence of the fur trade expanded into the Plains and the
articles it offered to the aborigines came to play an increasingly larger
role in the native economy and way of life, there developed needs for the
satisfaction of which it was necessary for the people to produce more and

[72] *Ibid.*, Vol. 2, p. 175.

[73] Bradbury purchased branded horses from the Arikara (Thwaites, 1906,
Vol. V, pp. 176—177). See also Umfreville, 1790, p. 178.

[74] Writing of the Sauk in Wisconsin (1740—75), Pond says that "Sometimes
they Go Near St. Fee in New Mexico and Bring with them Spanish Horseis,"
(original orthography, Pond, 1908, p. 335).

[75] Bradbury, in Thwaites, 1906, Vol. 5, p. 176, writes that the Arikara obtained their horses "... from the nations southwest of them, as the Cheyenne,
Poncars, Ponies, etc. who make predatory excursions in Mexico, and steal
horses from the Spaniards." Lewis and Clark also state that the Cheyenne
"... Steel horses from the Spanish Settlements, to the S.W. this excurtion
they make in one month..." (original orthography, Thwaites, 1904, Vol. 1,
p. 176).

[76] Grinnell, 1915, shows that a good deal of Cheyenne warfare involved
raiding for horses against these tribes.

[77] Although wild horses were captured whenever possible, and there was also
natural increase of the Indians' herds, these sources were insufficient for satis-
fying the demand for horses. Capturing and breaking wild horses was a relatively laborious and time-consuming process, whereas in trading and raiding
there was a certain amount of choice and opportunity for acquiring animals
already tamed for various purposes such as war, hunting, or transportation.
See also Mishkin, 1940, p. 6; and Grinnell, 1923b, Vol. I, pp. 291—295.

more of the goods used in exchange. The obvious superiority of guns, knives, axes, steel traps, metal for arrow points, brass kettles, etc., were immediately apparent to the natives, and their advantages in meeting the basic subsistence needs motivated the constant desire to secure them. Such trade implements were not only important as labor saving devices in the daily occupations of the aborigines, but were equally necessary in increasing the efficiency of production of goods used in the trade exchange: buffalo robes, beaver and other furs, dried meat, fat, etc. In addition, the trade also offered other new objects which were used for luxury, or prestige, or decorative purposes, the possession of which affected psychological or aesthetic needs, articles such as European clothing, beads, paints, colored cloths, brass wire, etc. The needs which the fur trade supplied may therefore be classified in two categories: first, the basic ones used in subsistence procurement; secondly, the luxury items for social and aesthetic purposes.

Tabeau (1803—1805) early recognized the significance of trade goods among the Plains Indians when he wrote, "It is evident that with the bow and arrow the Savages of the Upper Missouri can easily do without our trade, which becomes necessary to them only after it has created the needs."[78] And again, ". . . it is not to be doubted that custom, intercourse, the spirit of imitation, rivalry, the idea of luxury will give birth among the Savages to new needs; and the necessity of enjoying will produce the activity required to procure the means for them."[79]

Lest it be thought that the desire for satisfaction of certain wants among the Indians was indiscriminate, Stoddard dispels such an idea:

The Indians are much more particular in the color and quality of their goods than is generally suspected. Most of the tribes or nations differ in their choice of goods; and indeed they are always known to each other by their dresses. Whatever be their wants they will seldom purchase strouding, blankets, or any other articles, unless they be of the size, color, and quality, to which they are accustomed. They sometimes carry their fancy to such extremes as to involve themselves in distress; for they will endure the rigors of winter rather than cover their bodies with a blanket too large or too small, or which is deficient in a border, or has one too many, or the color of which is not suited to their taste.[80]

On the other hand, the extent to which the natives could become dependent upon European articles for the maintenance of existence is apparent in the case of the Plains Cree who

At the end of the first century of contact . . . are greatly dependent upon the (English and French) not only for arms, clothing and utensils, but even for provisions. From the self-sufficing plane of aboriginal existence, by 1740 they have passed into a state of economic subservience. They were specialists

[78] Tabeau in Abel, 1939, p. 72.
[79] *Ibid.*, p. 166.
[80] Stoddard, 1812, p. 299.

2

in fur trapping. The vagaries of the London and Paris fur markets directly touched the Indian in so far as they affected the returns he received for his labor. In addition to their dependence on the trader for articles which had become basic necessities, the Cree were perhaps more closely bound to the production of furs by their insatiable desires for liquor and tobacco.[81]

Another instance is a statement made at Fort Pitt in 1780 by representatives of some tribes to the Americans who were attempting to retain their loyalty during the Revolutionary War.

> If our father is allied to the Americans, why do these allow us to be in want of everything; must we die together with our wives and children while rejecting the offers which the English make to us; ...The wild animals which ought to nourish us and procure for us, by exchange of their skins, clothing to which we have become accustomed, are much more wild than they were before we made use of fire-arms. We are in need, therefore, of powder, of weapons, of traps, instead of the burning liquors which kill our young people, for that is all that is furnished to us...[82]

Changes in Hunting Patterns

The foregoing passage contains an interesting sidelight on some of the more subtle ecological or subsistence pattern changes resulting from the introduction of European instruments of production – in this case fire-arms. It is stated that the animals "are much more wild than they were before we made use of fire-arms," and it would therefore appear that the Indians' need of, and dependence upon, guns in the eastern forests was even deeper than it is usually thought to be. For, once animal "psychology" became affected by this innovation in hunting, the necessity for its continuance became practically absolute. It was essential for the bare maintenance of life, and rendered the bow and arrow relatively ineffective.

In the area of the Great Plains, on the other hand, the gun never attained such imperative importance in subsistence activity. As a matter of fact it was rarely used in hunting buffalo, and was actually prohibited by the Assiniboin on such occasions.[83] Though the rule in the hunt was not so stringent among the Mandan and Hidatsa, they gave a decided preference to the bow and arrow.[84]

[81] Mandelbaum, 1940, pp. 176—177.

[82] De la Balme to Luzerne, June 27, 1780, in Alvord, Clarence W., Kaskaskia Records, 1778—1790, Illinois State Historical Library Collections, Springfield, 1909, p. 164, quoted in Stevens, 1926, p. 55.

[83] Mc Donnell, 1889, Vol. I, p. 280. The loading of the cap-and-ball rifle of those days was a "meticulous and time-consuming task. The powder had to be measured and poured, the ball had to be rammed down the barrel with a long rod, the tube must be 'primed', and the cap or flint had to be adjusted. All this took about a minute... The Indian could in that time ride three hundred yards and discharge twenty arrows" (Webb, 1931, pp. 168—169).

[84] Mackenzie, 1889, Vol. I, p. 331; Wilson, 1924, p. 300.

Just as the gun among the forest tribes became a vital instrument of production once the process of its use was set in motion, so did the horse become a vital instrument of production among the Plains tribes. We have seen above how the dynamics of hunting and trade required that a continuous supply of horses be fed into the operation of those institutions. And in the case of hunting in particular this continuous supply of horses was essential to the maintenance of a changed tempo of action and habits which the use of those animals had engendered. Perrot's seventeenth century description of a buffalo surround on foot in which the entire population of a village participated contrasts strikingly with the relative ease of a similar performance by mounted hunters. According to Perrot, the operation began at midnight with the disposition of three columns of hunters, involved the utilization of old men, women and boys in setting fire to the grass, and necessitated breaking camp at a certain moment, with the final moving of the camp to the scene of carnage where the meat was distributed, cut up and dried. The activities of the entire population were thus centered on the hunt, which lasted approximately twelve hours.[85] The later equestrian hunters depended chiefly on the fleetness of their horses to seek out and chase the buffalo and then transport the kill back to the camp where the rest of the population was, in the meantime, free to pursue other required labors without interruption.

The extent to which the speed of a horse came to be relied upon in some instances is illustrated by the reason given to Captain Marcy by a Comanche chief for his refusal to sell his favorite horse.". . . if he were to sell him it would prove a calamity to his whole band, as it often required all the speed of this animal to insure success in the buffalo chase; that his loss would be felt by all his people. . ."[86]

Among the Plains Cree, "only a few men owned horses which were swift enough for the chase and trained to hunt buffalo. Fineday stated that about one tipi in ten would have a good buffalo horse. A number of families would attach themselves to the owner of such a horse and followed him wherever he moved his camp. They shared in the buffalo he was able to secure by means of his horse. Since these families were dependent on the horse owner for food, they were naturally quick to carry out his wishes or orders."[87]

Although some tribes, even after the advent of the horse, continued to build enclosures into which the buffalo were driven,[88] for the most part it was no longer necessary to expend the time and labor required for the erection of such structures once the horse became the primary instru-

[85] Perrot in Blair, 1911, Vol. 1, pp. 120—124.
[86] Marcy, 1937, p. 158.
[87] Mandelbaum, 1940, p. 195.
[88] Lewis, 1942, p. 35.

2*

ment of production among the Plains tribes. Some idea of the amount of time and labor involved in such construction which often engaged the efforts of the entire community,[89] may be gathered from the descriptions culled from the literature by Branch:

> One side of the trap used by the Blackfeet was formed by the vertical wall of a bluff; the other sides, six or eight feet high, were built of logs, rocks and brush. These walls did not have to be very strong, but they had to be tight enough that the buffalo could not see through them. From a point on the plateau overlooking the enclosure, piles of rock or clumps of bushes, placed at short intervals, extended outward like the outer ribs of a jaw . . .
> The Plains Crees, about the Qu'Appelle River, where there was much timber but no rocks, built a circular pen of tree trunks lashed together with green withes and braced by prop logs. Just under the gap in the circle the ground was sharply cut out, making a wall high enough to hold the buffalo from doubling back. Two rows of bushes, the wings of the chute, extended four miles out into the prairie . . .
> The Assiniboines built an enclosure in the open prairie. The fence was about four feet high and formed of strong stakes of birchwood, wattled with birch branches . . . As soon as the buffalo had been enticed within the pen, a screen of buffalo skins on a drop cord was let down across the opening.[90]

Changes in Labor Activity

Thus, the advent of the horse not only changed the patterns of the hunt, confining it more strictly to the active males, and eliminating certain previously required labors, but it also freed the other elements of the population, particularly the women, to direct their efforts in other channels. Reference was made above to Perrot's account of a buffalo hunt in which the women participated. Among the Blackfoot, too, when the buffalo were stampeded up the chute and into the pen, "the squaws and children were on the other side of the walls, whooping up a racket to keep the buffalo from pushing against the walls and escaping."[91]

With the elimination of the direct participation of women in this aspect of the culture, they were enabled to devote more time to fulfilling the requirements of the fur trade by preparing skins for market. This was hard and time-consuming labor. According to Briggs " . . . one squaw was capable of preparing ten (buffalo) robes in a season, although two or more worked together on the heavier ones."[92] The information given Fremont by an official of the American Fur Company stated that because of the difficulty of preparing and dressing the robes " . . . it is seldom that a lodge trades more than twenty skins in a year."[93] A Blackfoot chief told the Earl of Southesk "that his eight wives could dress a hundred and fifty skins in the year whereas a single wife could only dress ten . . ."[94]

[89] Lowie, 1909, p. 10.
[91] *Ibid.*, p. 36.
[93] Fremont, 1856, p. 255.

[90] Branch, 1929, pp. 35—37.
[92] Briggs, 1940, p. 142.
[94] Lewis, 1942, p. 39.

As far as the women were concerned, what the horse gave, the fur trade took away, for the latter only added to her burden of labor. The complex of historical factors changed her role as a producer from that of a participant in the old hunting pattern, to that of a worker in the fur trade. Without the proper dressing of the skins by the women, those articles were valueless for the market.

Just how the combined influences of the horse and the fur trade ultimately fostered an important increase in polygyny among the Blackfoot has been shown by Lewis, who writes that "... by 1833, the time when the large markets for tanned robes in the States first developed, there already existed an accumulation of horses that made possible the ensuing expansion of polygyny... men with large herds were the ones who could purchase many wives, and in the exchange thereby transform idle capital (surplus horses) into productive capital (women)."[95] Also, "After 1830, women captives were no longer sold or traded. They were now valued by the Blackfoot as an additional labor supply to meet the new needs of tanning hides and preparing provisions for the enormous market provided by the fur trade. Here again, the old importance of women in terms of numbers was overshadowed by their new importance as aids in the acquisition of the new equipment (guns, ammunition, etc.), that had become so necessary to Blackfoot life."[96]

Production of Surplus for Trade

Effective trade requires the production of a surplus beyond the needs of subsistence. The coming of the fur trade naturally stimulated such production to a far greater degree than aboriginal trade. And in the area of the northeastern Plains, along the Upper Missouri, this stimulus was felt by the forest tribes which impinged on the border of the Plains area; by the horticultural tribes of the Upper Missouri; and by the nomadic hunters west of the river. For it was through the villages of the Mandan, Hidatsa and Arikara that a great deal of the commerce passed.

The production of the forest tribes, consisting of furs, namely, beaver, was directly for the fur trade and, incidentally, also involved the exchange of fresh meat, wild rice, fat, syrup, and other products to the Whites engaged in the trade.[97]

Among the Plains groups, production of food for the fur trade assumed considerable proportions:

The Plains tribes came to be the chief providers of food for the far-flung fur trade, whose numerous posts extended throughout the Woodland area, the Barren Grounds, and along the Churchill, Columbia and Fraser Rivers. The Blackfoot, because of their control of the rich buffalo grounds became a

[95] *Ibid.*, p. 40. [96] *Ibid.*, p. 50.
[97] Pond, 1908, p. 347; Blair, 1911, Vol. I, p. 282.

major source of provisions. The fur traders of the forest regions above the North Saskatchewan depended upon those posts which were supplied with provisions by the Blackfoot, and whenever a shortage of food occurred, sent to them for assistance. The food trade consisted of large quantities of dried and pounded meat, pemmican, backfat and dried berries.[98]

Will and Hyde, in their study of the "corn culture" of the Indian tribes of the Upper Missouri region, devote an entire chapter to corn as an article of trade. They cite a number of references in the historical literature which exemplify the extent to which this was carried on with the Whites in corn and vegetables, and state that:

> ...this trade was certainly a great benefit (to the Indians) as it enabled them to procure much-coveted articles of European make; on the other hand it seems highly probable that the white explorers and traders would have found it impossible to carry on their operations without the supplies of food obtained from the village Indians... MacKinac Island, in the straights between Lake Huron and Lake Michigan, was a famous corn market of the early fur-traders. The great town of the Sacs on the Fox-Wisconsin River route to the Mississippi, was another center of this trade... Prairie du Chien on the Upper Mississippi was another center of the corn trade in early times; while on the Upper Missouri the villages of the Mandans, Hidatsas, Arikaras, and Omahas were the corn markets for parties going into the plains or to the Rocky Mountains.[99]

Although Hayden wrote approximately twenty years after the period with which we are here concerned, his information is, nevertheless, valid as an indication of a situation which had already been in existence for a considerable time. He writes as follows concerning the Arikara:

> Besides the great advantages accruing to themselves over other wandering tribes, by tilling the soil, they have two markets for their surplus produce. The first is the fort of the American Fur Company, located near their village, at which they trade from five hundred to eight hundred bushels in a season. This trade on the part of the Indians is carried on by the women, who bring the corn by panfuls or the squashes in strings, and receive in exchange knives, hoes, combs, beads, paints, etc.; also ammunition, tobacco, and other useful articles for their husbands... The second market for their grain is with several bands of the Dakotas, who are at peace with them. These Indians make their annual visits to the Arikaras, bringing buffalo robes, skins, meat, etc., which they exchange for corn; and the robes and skins thus obtained enable the Arikaras to buy at the trading-post the various cloths and cooking utensils needed by the women, and the guns, horses, etc. required by the men.[100]

At the same time some of the forest people produced sufficient to obtain a surplus of White trade goods which they employed in the native

[98] Lewis, 1942, pp. 28—29.
[99] Will and Hyde, 1917, pp. 191—192. See also, *ibid.*, footnote 13, p. 91, where the authors cite Major Marston (1820) to the effect that the Sac and Fox "... planted about 300 acres and grew about 8,000 bushels of corn each year, 1,000 bushels of which they sold to the white traders of Prairie du Chien."
[100] Hayden, 1863, pp. 353—354.

trade with the Missouri River village tribes. The latter, therefore, produced a surplus of agricultural staples which was exchanged not only with the forest tribes bordering the area, but also with the British traders who began coming into their vicinity in the latter part of the eighteenth century. In addition, and equally important, they had to provide garden produce for the nomadic hunters of the Plains, like the Crow and Cheyenne, who were also desirous of procuring vegetal foods.[101]

The incentive for the Plains tribes to come to the horticulturalists was by no means chiefly the desire to vary their meat diet. What they wanted were the articles of European manufacture which the village groups had accumulated from the White traders and the forest tribes. In this exchange the most important commodity they offered was horses, which were desired for use not only by the village peoples themselves, but also for their further exchange with the Assiniboin, Cree, Ojibwa and the Canadian traders,[102] from all of whom they acquired objects valued by the nomads. The latter had constantly to be engaged in the acquisition of horses by raiding from other tribes and from the Spanish ranches or presidios, or by trading the European goods secured from the villages.

A concatenation of trade events stimulated surplus production among various tribes which were mutually interdependent for the acquisition of commodities. Inasmuch as the products were passed from group to group, this surplus was produced for a market involving comparatively large numbers of tribes. This was an ever expanding process which, with the passage of time, developed ramifications and had repercussions radiating in all directions from the Plains, so that some Algonkian tribes, the eastern Dakota, the southwestern Plains tribes, the Mexican ranches, and the Plateau tribes were soon involved.

Mishkin has stated that, "Among Plains tribes there is a correlation between horse surpluses, trading and raiding. These three factors describe a circular course each maintaining and accelerating the other. Thus those tribes that owned surpluses were naturally the most active traders and in turn were compelled to be the most active raiders in order to replenish their surpluses for future trading."[103]

Although the correlation, stated by Mishkin, between horse surplus, trading and raiding, seems by and large to be true, it probably requires some qualification, as the evidence from the Comanche, who were probably the most active raiders of all the Plains tribes, does not entirely appear to bear it out. In spite of the fact that they possessed large herds of horses which they raided from the Spaniards, the Comanche do not appear to have been among the important trading tribes. According to some of the Spanish documents translated by Bolton, the Comanche, "...lacking the trade of the Europeans, and not devoting themselves to

[101] See the following chapter.   [102] Lewis, 1942, p. 29.
[103] Mishkin, 1940, p. 22.

agriculture, ... have no other clothing or food than that secured from
the wild cattle, which they follow... From these perpetual oscillations
(in following the buffalo herds) and such continual movement, they lose
a great many horses, for which loss they try to compensate themselves at
the expense of the ranches they encounter in Texas and Mexico...''[104]
And then again ''... (the Comanche being) in possession of such a territory that, finding in it an abundance of cattle which furnish them rai-
ment, food, and shelter, they only just fall short of possessing all of the
conveniences of the earth, and have no need to covet the trade pursued
by the rest of the Indians whom they call, on this account, slaves of the
Europeans, and whom they despise.''[105]

Nevertheless, the Comanche did engage in some trade, and, for the
weapons and agricultural products which they secured from the Wichita,
they exchanged horses, mules, and Apache captives, the latter to be sold
as slaves in Louisiana.

It would appear, then, that the loss of horses by the Comanche was
principally the result both of their use in the nomadic way of life and of
raids by other Plains tribes. The Comanche situation was rather unique
in that they formed a barrier between most of the Plains groups and the
Spaniards. In a sense they maintained a monopoly, and apart from the
Spanish, possessed the only other large horse herds in the Southwest.
Unless other tribes could get through to the Spanish they were compelled either to trade with, or raid from, the Comanche. Had the latter
really been interested in employing their herds for trading purposes they
could probably have become very wealthy, but the possession of much
property would have reduced their mobility and perhaps changed their
dominant position with respect to ownership of large herds. As it was,
the Comanche were content to secure weapons and agricultural food
through trade, and otherwise preferred to range through their territory
in hunting and warlike splendor.

On the other hand, those tribes that were farther away from the direct
source of supply of horses were dependent upon trading or were compelled to raid actively to maintain a surplus for the trade, and this was
true of the Cheyenne, Kiowa and Arapaho.

Relationship between Indian and European Economies

It might be well here to attempt briefly to visualize the role and
position of the Indian in the nexus of the economic complexities in which
he was involved. Only in the territory claimed by the Spanish Crown was
he subjected to the action of outright conquest or "pacification," and it
was this policy of attempting to make sedentary cultivators of extremely
mobile equestrian nomads which gave Spain so much trouble in the

[104] Bolton, 1914, Vol. 2, p. 174.   [105] *Ibid.*, Vol. 1, p. 219.

Southwest. Here Spain's problem was much different from any she had encountered among the aboriginal agriculturalists in Central and South America. She might well have been able to subdue the more sedentary of the river valley tribes on her northeastern frontier in the Louisiana Territory and parts of Texas, but the possession of the horse by those tribes, especially by the Comanche and Apache, in the latter part of her reign, gave the Indians a facile mobility which made it difficult for the Spanish governors and military to expedite the Crown policy. Furthermore, in spite of the fact that ". . . the narrow commercial policy of the Spanish government permitted trade with the Indians only under the strictest regulations and entirely prohibited supplying them with firearms,"[106] this attempt at rigid control was vitiated by the ability of the Indians to secure their desired objects of trade from the French and even from the English. This latter situation was a reflection of the differences in colonial and imperial policies in North America between Spain on the one hand and France and Britain on the other. In the case of Spain, it is true that she had no lands rich in fur-bearing animals as did the other two nations; but the important point is that "it was the Spanish Crown itself which took the initiative in exploiting and conquering America."[107] As a consequence, all her efforts were directed toward the establishment of a feudal system based on ownership by Spanish lords of land worked by "unpaid, forced, Indian labor for life:" the encomienda. In the case of England and France, however, the sovereigns delegated "the initiation and development of overseas empire chiefly to business organizations. . . The result was of profound importance in making the story of the frontier different in North America from that of Latin America."[108]

The business organizations were obviously interested in profits, and it was from the fur trade that they were derived. The policies pursued by the mercantile interests of France and Britain were therefore predicated on the maintenance of a "free" labor supply, such as that offered by the aborigines who were already skilled and experienced in the hunting of animals whose skins the Europeans were most interested in securing. They already had at hand ". . .the cheapest and best supply of born hunters of these animals. . ."[109] and so the Indians were made use of as independent producers while their tribes were dealt with as independent sovereign states. "The Indian hunters spent their labour as free men roaming the woods, and brought back furs which they traded off to the French (or English) for objects they themselves desired. The labour of these free Indians was ultimately productive of profits to the French (or English) fur traders; and this was about all that the (trading interests) wanted. Neither in Russian nor French (nor British) North America, therefore, was enslavement of the Indians either economically or

[106] *Ibid.*, Vol. 1, pp. 40, 270.   [107] Macleod, 1928, p. 127.
[108] *Ibid.*, p. 129.   [109] *Ibid.*, p. 149.

politically expedient."[110] The British and French "...regarded the
Indian lands as hunting grounds which were to be retained as such to
supply furs for foreign markets. This purpose coincided with the desires
of the Indians; it enabled them to keep their ancestral homes and to
engage in their accustomed occupations."[111]

In terms of the organization of the British trade, then, which may be
cited as an example, the Indian was at the ultimate end of a chain, or
better still, at the lowest stratum of a business system in which he
played the most important role: that of the producer. Next above him
was the White trader with whom he exchanged his furs for European
articles. This trader secured his goods or worked for the next higher
stratum, that of the merchants who were located at Detroit or Michilli-
mackinac. These men were usually middlemen for the highest level of
merchant, represented by the great firms of Montreal. Beyond them
were the London houses who transacted business in the markets of
Europe.[112]

[110] *Ibid.*, p. 300.   [111] Tohill, 1928, p. 45.
[112] See Stevens, 1926, Chapter V, especially pp. 122—124.

CHAPTER TWO

THE PLAINS TRADE SITUATION

The tribal groups in the Northern Plains were situated between two great primary sources of trade goods entering the area from opposite points of the compass. From the southwestern periphery came the supply of horses, and from the northeast, where the British traders were located, came the supply of European manufactures. The important parties effecting the transport and exchange of goods were the horse nomads such as the Cheyenne, who travelled long distances to the mercantile centers of the Upper Missouri villages, bringing their goods and carrying others away. What was brought away was passed from tribe to tribe in further exchanges in the interior Plains. But it was the agricultural villages of the Upper Missouri that were the focus of interests converging there from the northeast and southwest for the purposes of trade.

Two basic divisions may be made in the trade: first, that which took place between Indian and White, and secondly, that between Indian and Indian. In the first division, the Whites engaged in direct trade with aborigines of three different subsistence types: forest hunting tribes, agricultural village tribes, and buffalo hunting horse nomads. In the second division, trade between Indians, the exchanges took place with the villages as the center of the transactions. The latter traded with some forest tribes on the one hand and with the Plains nomads on the other. In Canada, however, exchanges did take place between Plains nomads and forest tribes, but those central and southern Plains tribes with which we are primarily concerned had no direct contact with the forest hunters.

Trade between Indian and European

Whites and forest tribes. The commercial relations between Europeans and Indians of the forests of eastern North America form a major part of the history of the fur trade in the New World. This subject has been dealt with exhaustively by a number of scholars,[1] and no attempt is made to summarize here a vastly complex situation which, in its details, is not directly relevant to the problem under consideration. This trade is important for present purposes chiefly as a channel for the introduction of European goods into the stream of Plains intertribal trade and to indicate briefly the nature of the direct trade contacts between the

[1] See for example Innis, 1930; and Morton, n. d.

Whites and forest tribes as one subdivision of the categories outlined in the preceding section of this chapter. The subject is, therefore, confined to a brief, largely generalized, statement applicable to both British and French relations with the Indian producers of furs.

During the monopolistic regime of the Hudson's Bay Company forest hunters journied to the factories of that establishment with their skins. Great distances were involved in hazardous trips which often resulted in loss of life to the Indians, and which took months to complete. But after the field was entered by other traders, and the era of competition began, individual White traders took their outfit of goods with them into the interior, and did their business in the tribal territories. This relieved the aborigines of the necessity of time-consuming journeys. The large fur-trading companies then established forts at various points in the interior and either the traders undertook their expeditions from these forts or the Indians themselves came to the forts to trade.

The individual trader who established a post in the interior of the forest area would make contact with the natives, inform them of the goods he had and the prices of them in terms of furs, chiefly beaver skins. If the hunters had furs on hand they could effect exchanges immediately and also be given credits for a certain number of skins which they promised to bring later in the season or the following winter when the trader returned. The amount of credit an individual hunter would receive depended on his known skill as a hunter and also on his integrity. In some instances, the leader of a band would assume responsibility for insuring a return on the credits extended to the hunters in his group.[2]

Whites and village tribes. In the case of the village tribes, the traders of the Hudson's Bay and Northwest Companies who visited them as competitors, were faced with a somewhat different situation inasmuch as they were not dealing with direct producers. The Upper Missouri Indians obtained their furs mainly through trade with the various nomadic hunters who came from the west (Crows, Flathead) and southwest (Cheyenne, Arapaho, Kiowa) of their establishments. As far as the amount of furs which they acquired in this manner is concerned, it was apparently substantial and profitable enough to make the agricultural-ists feel that it was not worth their while to take the trouble involved in hunting beaver and other animals. According to Charles Mackenzie, a trader of the Northwest Company, who was among the Mandan and Hidatsa in 1804, "Beavers are plentiful, but the Indians will not take the trouble of attending to them. They often remarked to me that they would think it a pleasure to supply us with beavers if they could be secured the same as buffaloes by a chase on horseback, but they con-

[2] For detailed descriptions of the manner in which this trade was carried on see the following sources: Umfreville, 1790; Pond, 1908; Harmon, 1903; Peirault, 1909, 1910, pp. 508—619.

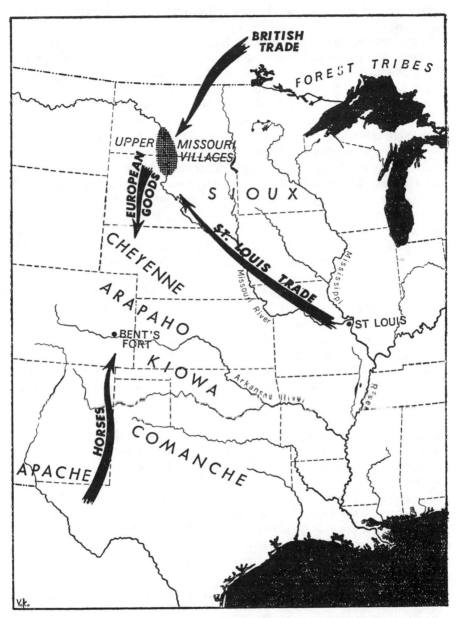

Map 2. Flow of European Commodities into Tribal Areas.

sidered the operation of searching for them in the bowels of the earth to satisfy the avarice of the Whites, not only troublesome but very degrading."[3]

Furthermore, the agriculturalists had another advantage in that they produced a regular and more or less dependable surplus of crops for which the traders exchanged their goods.[4] McDonnell, in writing of the Mandans during the period 1793—1797, states that "they raise indian corn or maize, beans, pumpkins, squashes in considerable quantity, not only sufficient to supply their own wants, with the help of the buffalo but also to sell and give away to all strangers that enter their villages."[5] David Thompson, who was among the same Indians in 1797 writes: "The produce they raise (is) not only enough for themselves, but also for trade with their neighbors. We brought away upwards of 300 pounds weight."[6] Stoddard, referring to the period between 1804 and 1812, says of the Pawnee that they ". . . raise more than double the quantity of corn and vegetables than is necessary for their own consumption, and furnish their neighbors with the surplus in exchange for peltries; so that their trade, which is now engrossed by the Spaniards, is deemed of considerable value."[7] If the supply of horses was not entirely dependable, it was at least an additional commodity by means of which the village tribes obtained European articles. Thus, in their trade with the Whites they functioned both as middlemen and direct producers. The furs and horses were obtained in trade with the Plains nomads, while the food crops were the results of their own efforts.

It would appear that in the trade relations between the village Indians and White traders, the chiefs and headmen were the important intermediaries, and often one of the latter was instrumental in securing trade for representatives of one of the large companies towards whom he happened to be favorably disposed. In one instance related by Mackenzie, he had arrived at a village after some Hudson's Bay men had been there and secured the advantage. One important Indian with whom he stayed, apparently not wishing to discourage other traders from coming there, told Mackenzie not to worry, he would get him furs. The elder then "himself went upon the top of a house and harangued in our favor, while his kind females were busily employed from place to place collecting the skins until the whole was thus secured."[8]

[3] Mackenzie in Masson, 1889, p. 331.

[4] See the previous chapter on production of surplus for trade. Will and Hyde, call attention to the fact that during the winter which Lewis and Clark spent among the Mandan the explorers used several hundred bushels of corn (1917, p. 146).

[5] McDonnell in Masson, 1889, p. 273.

[6] Thompson in Tyrrell, 1916, pp. 231—232.

[7] Stoddard, 1812, p. 456.

[8] Mackenzie in Masson, 1889, p. 334.

Bradbury's account of the trading which took place in 1810 between the Arikara and Hunt and Lisa is interesting for its details of the preliminary council and the manner of bargaining toward an agreed price. The chief of the Arikara village, Le Gauche,

> opened the council by a short speech: in the first place he spoke of their poverty, but said that they were very glad to see us, and would be still more glad to trade with us. Lisa replied, and expressed his intention to trade, if they did not rate their buffaloe and beaver too highly... Mr. Hunt declared that the object of his journey was not to trade, but to see our brothers at the great salt lake in the west; for that undertaking he should now want horses, as he purposed to go thence by land, and that he had plenty of goods to exchange, if they would spare the horses. Mr. Lisa and Mr. Hunt accompanied their speeches by suitable presents of tobacco. Le Gauche spoke and expressed the satisfaction of his people at our coming, and their attachment to the white men. In respect to the trade with Mr. Lisa, he wished for more time to fix the price of dried buffaloe skins, (usually called buffaloe robes) being an article they had most of: his present idea of the price was thirty loads of powder and ball for each robe. Respecting Mr. Hunt's proposition, he was certain they could not spare the number of horses that he understood he wanted; and that he did not think they ought to sell any horses. Les Yeux Gris, another chief, replied to the latter part of his speech by stating that they might easily spare Mr. Hunt a considerable number of horses, as they could readily re-place them by stealing or by smoking. These arguments governed the opinions of the chiefs and it was determined to open a trade for horses, when they were satisfied with the price Mr. Hunt proposed to give. The council now broke up, ...
>
> ... the morning being rainy, no business was done in the village until the afternoon, when Mr. Hunt exhibited the kind and quantity of goods purposed to give for each horse. These were placed in the lodge of Le Gauche, for general inspection, and proved to be satisfactory.
> ... I understood that Lisa and the chiefs had agreed that the price of a buffalo robe should be twenty balls, and twenty loads of powder. He removed a part of his goods to the lodge of Le Gauche, and Mr. Hunt began to trade at the lodge of the Big Man. The trade for horses soon commenced: the species of goods most in demand were carbines, powder, ball, tomahawks, knives, etc. as another expedition against the Sioux was meditated.[9]

Thus, prices were agreed to by the traders and the chiefs, with the actual business being done in the lodges of the latter.

Whites and nomads. Below the Canadian border, there was comparatively little direct trade between the Plains nomads and the fur traders because the market was not a dependable one for the reasons ably and succintly summarized by Tabeau. It must be borne in mind, that although there was a developing trade in buffalo robes, yet, in the first quarter of the nineteenth century, while the beaver returns were declining, it was still the fur most in demand by the traders. It was then, still on a basis of a desire for beavers that Tabeau penned the following remarks in support of his opinion that trade with the nomadic tribes could not be profitable:

[9] Bradbury in Thwaites, 1906, Vol. 5, pp. 130—132.

1st. All the wandering nations which subsist on the buffalo do not dwell very long in the places suitable to the beaver, the otter, and the bear, all animals hostile to the prairies.

2nd. They disregard all other hunting and are unskillfull at it.

3rd. The facility of buffalo hunting with the arrow, as it requires only going to meet the animals, makes them dislike all fatigue. The beaver can be obtained only by activity and industry as they are nowhere common enough to be hunted with the arrow or the gun.

4th. None of these nations values our merchandise highly and, if we except some iron implements, they have more liking for their skins, white as alabaster, which they work upon and ornament in different ways and which are, throughout the Upper Missouri, the foremost fancy goods.

5th. They find in the buffalo cow, as I have elsewhere remarked, everything necessary to them and much that is superfluous, and, for this hunt, they rightly prefer the bow and arrow to our guns and ammunition. If they desire the latter, it is for war alone, as they do not even dare use them against the black bear which is very common in the Black Hills.[10]

Actually, although the nomads caught beaver, they did not know how to trap the animals or dress them properly. Every time the Cheyenne met traders, which was a relatively infrequent occurrence, they never had enough beaver to impress them and usually asked for Whites to be sent into their country to teach them how to catch beaver and to trade with them.

Although a trader named Guenneville spent a disappointing winter in 1804—05 with the Cheyenne in the Black Hills, he was not, as Tabeau says, the first trader among them. Certainly Trudeau in 1795 traded a few skins from them, and he had been preceded among them by a few months by Jacques D'Eglise. At least the latter brought back two French-Canadian traders, one of whom had wintered among the Cheyenne, in 1794—95, who were situated in the vicinity of the Arikara villages.[11] At any rate, Tabeau has this to say about Guenneville's sojourn with the Cheyenne:

> ... Guenneville, having left the village of the Ricaras the 11th of August, 1804, followed the Cheyennes in all their ramblings in the neighborhood of the Black Hills and elsewhere and assured me on his arrival the 11th of April that on going and returning he did not see beaver three times. His trading has brought him only eighty-four pounds and he did not leave one in the hands of the Savages, who, meeting a trader for the first time, surpassed themselves in the hunt ... the beaver and the otter cannot become objects of trade with the hunters, the Sioux and the Ricaras, at least from the River Qui Court (Niobrara) up to the Mandans inclusively; for I understand that these could scarcely furnish them for the English companies..."[12]

When in August, 1806, Lewis and Clark were in the Arikara villages on their return journey, there was a camp of 120 Cheyenne lodges situated nearby. One of the chiefs "requested me to send some traders to

---

[10] Tabeau in Abel, 1939, pp. 162—163.   [11] Nasatir, 1927, p. 69.
[12] Tabeau in Abel, 1939, p. 87.

them, that their country was full of beaver and they would then be encouraged to kill beaver, but now they had no use for them as they could get nothing for their skins and did not know well how to catch beaver. If the white people would come amongst them they would become acquainted and they would learn them how to take beaver."[13]

Henry, who had been among them a month previous writes that "what few beaver skins they had were purchased without much trouble; but grizzly bear skins they value highly, and will take and return payment ten times before you can get one."[14] He goes on to say: "They sometimes dispose of their skins to the Pawnee (Arikaras ?) and Sioux; or if they find any traders from the Islenois (Illinois River) they deal with them."[15]

Again the Cheyenne apparently are attempting to lure traders into their country with tales of abundant furs and cheap prices.

> They informed us that last fall two Spaniards came up the river which runs to the South, in a wooden canoe or a boat loaded with goods, who passed the winter among them, disposed of all their property, and sold very cheap, giving a large double handful of gunpowder and 50 balls for one beaver. They told us that by Spring the two men had collected such a quantity of skins that they were obliged to make another canoe;...[16]

On the other hand, Charles Mackenzie was among them at the same time as Henry, and although he had no more than £ 5 worth of inferior goods, he considered himself very successful when he wrote "... I sold the few articles I had to advantage, having got about a hundred weight of beaver, four of the finest bear skins I had ever seen, with some fine buffalo robes."[17] It should be mentioned, however, that there were also some Arapaho and Sioux among the Cheyenne, and the total production of beaver may not have come entirely from the Cheyenne.

In 1812, Luttig recorded in his journal that among the furs, tongues, meat and moccasins traded by twenty-six lodges of Cheyenne, there were seventy-five beaver skins, which would average less than three skins to a lodge.[18]

It is obvious that there was not and could not be any profitable trade in beaver — that is, profitable both to trader and to Plains nomad. Since there was little inducement for traders to attempt to follow the horse Indians into the Interior Plains, there resulted a tendency for the Cheyenne and others to bring their "peltry" to the village tribes where they could at the same time trade for food staples and European goods. The situation was thus one of maximum efficiency of effort on both sides, for the trader could then secure his furs at designated places. Although

[13] Thwaites, 1904, Vol. V, p. 357.   [14] Henry in Coues, 1897, p. 383.
[15] Ibid., p. 384.   [16] Ibid.
[17] Mackenzie in Masson, 1889, p. 381.
[18] Luttig, 1920, p. 100. Luttig's other references to trade with the Cheyenne mention only "2 beavers" (p. 92) and "some beaver" (p. 86).

village Indians were much shrewder traders, it was nevertheless generally easier for the Whites to deal with them than with the Interior Plains tribes. In the case of the Crow, Mackenzie says in 1805: "Afraid to ask too small a price, they seemed averse from dealing with me, for they would have a white man pay four times the value of a thing, or often let him go without."[19] The Cheyenne, however, must have learned their obstinate trade practices from the Arikaras, and they made life doubly difficult for Tabeau by advising the tribes they brought along with them. He implies that the Cheyenne had more experience in trade than we would ordinarily think. This should not be too surprising, perhaps, as they came out of the northeast where the fur trade was very intense. Tabeau writes:

> Now that the Cheyennes have ceased to till the ground, they roam over the prairies west of the Missouri on this side of the Black Hills, from which they come regularly at the beginning of August to visit their old and faithful allies, the Ricaras. The Cheyennes, who have always visited either the Whites or the Savages of the St. Peter's (Minnesota) River, are, at least, as difficult to trade with as the Ricaras, and a man, Guenneville, who came from among them, says nothing good of them. The nation has only a half knowledge of the value of merchandise and prides itself, none the less, on being ignorant in this respect. This vain-glory has been conducive to my detriment in the slight trade of the Caninanbiches (Arapaho) and others who obstinately defer to its judgment ... it is certain, that if it had not been for the interference of the Cheyennes, I should have made better use of the nations who accompanied them this year for the first time on their visit to the Ricaras. They would probably have left to my discretion the price of the trifles they brought...[20]

What is truly surprising in this passage is that the Cheyenne "have always visited either the Whites or the Savages of the St. Peter's River," for all the information extant points to the fact that it was the Sioux who monopolized this source of trade.

Whites and Cheyenne. It would appear that the first attempt by a European to place the Cheyenne trade on an organized basis was made by Trudeau in the Spring of 1795 when he summoned the important men of "both Cheyenne villages" and "asked them to choose from among their number, the one whom they deemed most worthy to wear the medal and to be made the great chief of their nation. They had me give it to a young man who they called 'the Lance', who accepted it and promised to do all the good which had been recommended to him..."[21] However, this young man was a tyrant to his own people and to strangers, committed murder and had stolen horses from the Mandan and Hidatsa. Aside from the fact that he was denounced and reproached by the old men, we know nothing of what happened to him. In any event there is no record of the exact process of trade which took place, though Trudeau, Tabeau, Mackenzie, Hunt, etc., speak of it.

[19] Mackenzie in Masson, 1889, p. 346.   [20] Tabeau in Abel, 1939, p. 153.
[21] Trudeau, 1914, p. 472.

When Mackenzie was in a camp of Cheyenne preliminary to their making peace with the Hidatsa in 1806, he was taken by one of the chiefs to his tent. "My host, after giving me to eat of the best which his lodge and the camp could afford, made a long harangue commanding those who had furs to come and trade them ... which they readily obeyed, so that before sunset I had not a single article remaining..."[22]

Luttig's Journal, kept in 1812 at Fort Manuel in South Dakota, indicates that when a Cheyenne band arrived at that establishment it was the chiefs who entered the post to learn what there was to trade, and informed the Whites of the quantity and kinds of articles which they had at their camp. In one instance, they contemptuously observed that the post "had not Goods enough for their Peltries..." The information was carried back to camp and then the people came to the fort to trade.

After the establishment of Bent's Fort on the Arkansas River, when the Cheyenne camped in the vicinity of the trading post, the chiefs would ask that particular traders be sent to them.

> When the trader reached an Indian camp he went to the lodge of a chief or principal man, with whom he stayed and under whose protection he placed his goods. Soon after his arrival the crier went about the camp calling out the news of the trader's arrival, announcing what goods he had brought and what he wished to trade for. Thus, when Garrard visited the Cheyenne camp with Smith, the crier called out that Smith had come to trade for mules, and had brought tobacco, blue blankets, black (deep blue) blankets, white blankets, coffee, etc.[23]

At that period the trade was in buffalo robes, horses and mules, the Indians invariably paying for the goods with those animals.

Tribal Attempts to Monopolize European Trade

The tribes all along the length of the Missouri invariably attempted to prevent the progress of the White traders further than their own villages. Each tribe wished as far as possible to retain control of the White trade and to prevent the goods, especially guns, from flowing freely into the coffers of other tribes. Although they may not have been entirely averse to the European articles falling into the hands of other groups, their desire was nevertheless to regulate the amount that did so in accordance with their own benefit and wishes. So long as they retained the trade advantage and a superiority over other tribes and they could dispose of the goods as they saw fit, they were willing to share the bounty – unequally. This intent was obviously at variance with the interests of the traders, who were desirous of reaching as wide a market as they could supply and, through competition among the tribes for their wares, of

[22] Mackenzie in Masson, 1889, p. 381.   [23] Grinnell, 1923a, p. 58.

3*

purchasing furs as cheaply as possible. The Indians were not unaware of this elementary economic principle and were as interested in creating the conditions of a seller's market with respect to furs as were the traders in maintaining a buyer's market. In short, they realized the advantages of monopoly control; and if they could regulate the supply of furs coming into the hands of the trader they could buy his goods cheaply. Furthermore, what they could not achieve through peaceful methods, they were willing to obtain by means of force. Consequently, when they did not have sufficient commodities to purchase the entire stock of a trader's outfit, they attempted to persuade him to remain among them until they could bring in enough furs to do so; or failing that, they appropriated his goods. This was done either by outright seizure or by compelling him to "sell" his goods at a price so ridiculously cheap that it was tantamount to robbery.

For one thing, each tribe wished to prevent guns from falling into the hands of their enemies, and this was undoubtedly the most important interest the Indians had in attempting to control the trade. Superiority in firearms would obviously enable any tribe to maintain the balance of power in its international relations. For another, each tribe wished to act in the capacity of a middleman and have others dependent upon it for European supplies at least. If a tribe could buy up the furs of another cheaply, then it could profit in the exchange with the trader by closing off another outlet for his goods which could then be purchased at an advantage.

When, in 1794, Trudeau made his way up the Missouri in an effort to reach the trade of the Arikara, he had to run a gauntlet of tribes who were interested in obstructing his passage. In the beginning of his account, he first mentions the experience the French have had with the Omaha and Ponca:

> The trade in pelts with (the Ponca) would be advantageous were it not that the Omahas, although their allies, offer an obstacle hindering the traders from reaching there in the Autumn, suffering them only rarely to go in the Spring to make an exchange of such merchandise as remains after they have taken out at least the better part.
> They never failed to try to persuade the French that it was for the conservation of their profit and the safety of their lives that they retained them, saying that this people called the Poncas were not civilized, that they only think of robbing, striking, or killing those who entered their country and because of the great friendship which they had for the French they did not wish any evil to befall them; false talk which they gave us. The real motive which urges them to act is their own interest, for in depriving this nation of a direct commerce with us they would obtain all the best pelts, beaver and otter, for a mere bagatelle, which they sold again very dear, and they exchange these same pelts either with us or with nations situated on the Mississippi for good merchandise which they obtain very cheap.[24]

[24] Trudeau, 1914, p. 413.

Tabeau also recounts an incident in which Loisel was stopped by some Sioux bands along the Missouri, and he resolved the difficult situation by telling them that he would retain the merchandise for their trade the following winter. Whereupon one of the chiefs left with his band "to seek the Cheyennes upon the branches of the Fork, so that he might trade with them for the beaver which he supposed they had and which they had not, and to bring it to the Isle of Cedars, where Mr. Loisel..." would trade with them for the furs.[25]

In this particular instance, there might have been no great difficulty had it not been for the obstinacy of an "old soldier." Inasmuch as the goods were destined for "the Saones and Okondones at the Fork" (Teton bands on the Cheyenne River), he refused to let the trading party proceed because one of those bands had stolen some of his horses. In addition, he was angry with Loisel for having previously refused his daughter in marriage. The chiefs, however, were in favor of permitting the party to pass, though they were apparently powerless because as Tabeau says, "Among the Titons the chiefs have authority only when it is a question of pillage; but if it is a question of calming a riot, or stopping pillage, or aiding a trader in his expedition, all authority was nought before the opposition of a single individual."[26]

The chiefs were, however, apparently concerned with the effect the stopping of the goods would have upon the other bands of Sioux for whom they were destined, and they represented strongly that

> ... they have already only too many foreign enemies without alienating their own nation by a procedure so unjust; that the Titons of the Fork, the Cheyennes, and others, who are on the point of going there, would not fail to avenge the insult and the wrong which would be done them by stopping the merchandise which is destined for them; and that, furthermore, their tribe alone being incapable of furnishing enough peltries for all the merchandise of the trader, the French would withdraw discontented.[27]

The Arikara, too, were practicing restraint of trade as early as 1796, as we learn from Evans's Journal: "... the Rik, karas would not permit me to pass their village and carry my goods to those nations that reside above them, they said, they were themselves in want of Goods, etc. finding then that all my efforts were in vain to get on, I was obliged to stay among them." While there, several weeks later, the Cheyenne and Arapaho "came to the village to see me. Their chief in a very long and prolix discourse expressed to me the joy they felt to see the Whites. They assured me of the Love and Attachment for their Great Father the Spaniard and for all his children who came in their country."[28]

The Assiniboin, who traded both at the posts of the North West Company and at the villages of the Mandan and Hidatsa, greatly

[25] Tabeau in Abel, 1939, p. 140.   [26] *Ibid.*, pp. 105—106.
[27] *Ibid.*, p. 107.   [28] Quaife, 1916, p. 196.

resented the traders engaging the commerce of the agriculturalists directly. La Rocque, while on his way to the Upper Missouri villages in 1804, met a returning party of Assinboin, and he writes:

> ... if they were numerous enough, they would endeavor to pillage us of our goods, it being their fixed determination to prevent, as much as they can, any communication between the traders and the Missouri Indians, as they wish to engross that trade themselves.[29]

When the Mandans in 1805 opposed the progress of the same trader for exploratory purposes up the Missouri, they were quite frank in the reasons they offered for their refusal to permit him to proceed. "They asserted that if the white people would extend their dealings to the Rocky Mountains, the Mandanes would thereby become great sufferers, as they would not only lose all the benefit which they had hitherto derived from their intercourse with these distant tribes, but that in measure as these tribes obtained arms, they would become independent and insolent in the extreme."[30] The Crow in particular were among the most important customers of the Mandan.

In 1806, Mackenzie was approached by some Cheyenne peace ambassadors to the Hidatsa to accompany them on the return to their camp for the purpose of trading, but the Hidatsa were opposed to this and "would not hear of my going there with goods, but concealed their real motives under pretense of my personal safety."[31]

In 1807, Manuel Lisa, on his way up the Missouri from St. Louis with a keelboat full of trade goods, had to run a gauntlet of tribes consisting first of Arikara, then Mandan, and finally Assiniboin, all of whom had learned of his coming and were prepared to use force against him and his party. It was only Lisa's alertness, combined with the number of his musketry and swivel guns, which enabled him to continue his passage after trading with the Indians.[32]

In 1810, two hundred and eight lodges of Sioux had been waiting on the Missouri for eleven days at a point north of Chamberlain, South Dakota, for Hunt's party "with a decided intention of opposing our progress, as they would suffer no one to trade with the Ricaras, Mandans and Minaterees (Hidatsa), being at war with those nations."[33] When the party arrived at the Arikara villages above Grand River, "the interpreter informed us that the chiefs had come to a resolution to oppose our farther progress up the river, unless a boat was left to trade with them."[34]

This practice of interfering with the passage of traders along the river was not confined to the Missouri only. Major Long writes of an arrangement he saw in 1817 at a Sioux village on the east bank of the Mississippi above the St. Croix.

[29] La Rocque in Masson 1889, p. 301.   [30] Mackenzie in Masson, 1889, p. 343.
[31] Ibid. p. 375.   [32] Chittenden, 1935, Vol. I, Chap. IV.
[33] Bradbury in Thwaites, 1906, p. 103   [34] Ibid., p. 128.

One of their cabins is furnished with loop holes, and is situated so near the water that the opposite side of the river is within musket shot range from this building. By this means the Petit Corbeau (chief of the village) is enabled to exercise a command over the passage of the river, and has in some instances compelled traders to land with their goods, and induced them, probably through fear of offending him, to bestow presents to a considerable amount before he would suffer them to pass.[35]

It is thus apparent that everywhere along the Missouri attempts were made by all the village Indians to prevent traders from selling their goods directly to other tribes. Although, as we have seen, the Assiniboin also engaged in this practice, the various bands of the Teton Dakota were the chief nomadic groups who followed this procedure, and were aptly called "the pirates of the Missouri." Actually they earned the appelation not so much for their aggressions against the traders as for the depredations they practiced against the Upper Missouri Indians.[36]

Trade between Indian Groups

Forest and village tribes. We have seen that the forest tribes whose territories impinged upon the northeastern periphery of the Plains at the Upper Missouri villages acted, to some extent, in the capacity of middlemen between the Canadian traders and the village tribes. This medium for the introduction of European goods into the Plains was functioning for some time before the advent of White traders among the agriculturalists in the latter part of the eighteenth century. As early as 1736, Father Aulneau referred to the annual trade of corn, which took place between the Assiniboin and the Mandan,[37] and although the Cree are not actually mentioned in this connection until later, it is highly probable that they, too, participated in this trade at that early date, because of their close alliance with the Assiniboin. Specific accounts of trade between tribes north of the Missouri and those living on that river exist only for the Assiniboin and Mandan, though references are made to the fact that the Cree and Ojibwa also came to the villages to trade.

> Within one hundred years after the arrival of the whites, the Cree moved westward. The fur trade impelled the movement, the gun enabling them to push other people before them. They were brought to the fringes of the prairie country in their quest for fresh fur-trapping areas. Because of their function as middlemen in the trade they travelled into the Plains to carry trade goods to distant tribes. Their superior armament enabled them to gain a foothold in the plains.[38]

Mackenzie, in 1805, writes that "Several bands of Assiniboines, Crees and Sauteux Ojibwa visited the Hidatsa villages."[39] Mandelbaum,

---

[35] Long, 1860—67, p. 31.
[36] See below, the discussion on the relations of the Sioux with other tribes.
[37] Thwaites, 1900, Vol. 68, p. 293.
[38] Mandelbaum, 1940, p. 152.   [39] Mackenzie in Masson, 1889, p. 351.

referring to Lewis and Clark's attempt, in 1804, to halt the trade going on between the Cree and the Mandan, writes as follows: "Although the Americans recount a ceremony of adoption and an exchange of property between the Assiniboin and the Cree and Mandan, they wrote as though the allies had a sinister hold upon the village dwellers, i. e., the Mandans. They argued that the Mandan should trade with the Americans and not with the native middlemen..."[40]

The Assiniboin-Mandan[41] exchange of specific articles is first mentioned in the Verendrye Journal of 1738—39.[42] The trade that took place was on the basis of European goods – guns, powder, bullets, kettles, axes, knives, awls – provided by the Assiniboin who received in turn from the Mandan such articles of aboriginal production as corn, tobacco, "peltry," dyed plumes, painted buffalo robes, well-tanned skins of deer and "buck" decorated with fur and feathers, dyed plumes, quill worked garters, head bands, and belts. It is to be noted here that an agricultural tribe is exchanging products of the hunt – peltry, painted buffalo robes, well-tanned skins of deer and buck. Unfortunately, nowhere are the quantities of the various goods mentioned by Verendrye. It would be interesting to know them in view of the statement made to Verendrye by an Assiniboin spokesman about the Mandan that "most of the time they have neither meat nor fat." It was on this account that the Assiniboin accompanying Verendrye to the Mandans hunted buffalo on the way so that they would have sufficient fat to eat with the corn they would get there. As the Assiniboin statement is probably true, the question arises as to just how much "peltry," buffalo, or deerskins the Mandan could produce by their own efforts. Will and Hyde seem to think that before the acquisition of guns and horses by the Upper Missouri tribes

> hunting on foot with bows and arrows, spears and clubs, the kills must have been small ... herds large enough to make (surround) hunting profitable probably did not often come near enough to the villages to make the transportation of the meat on dogs and human backs possible. It is hardly likely that the kills in a region continuously occupied by a large fixed population could have been very frequent, nor that the supplies of meat obtained could have furnished even half of the sustenance of the people.[43]

The most important commodity in the exchange, other than furs and skins of various kinds, was undoubtedly corn, and it may well be that

[40] Mandelbaum, 1940, pp. 182—183.
[41] In calling the Mantannes of the Verendrye Journal of 1738—39 Mandans I am following the customary usage of previous writers. However, Mr. O. G. Libby, editor of the North Dakota Historical Quarterly, in the introduction to a new translation of the Journal by Henry E. Haxo, 1941, (pp. 229—241) argues cogently that the Mantannes, of which Verendrye writes, are in reality the Hidatsa. This distinction, however, is not important for the present discussion.
[42] *Ibid.*, pp. 242—271.   [43] Will and Hyde, 1917, pp. 144—145.

this was the mainstay of the trade. The remaining items in the inventory – garters, belts, head bands, feathers – could hardly have been of any great consequence.

According to Verendrye "the Mantannes dress skins more skillfully than any of the other tribes and they also do work in fur and feathers very tastefully, which the Assiniboines are not able to do."[44] In view of what Henry says less than sixty years later with regard to trade between the Cheyenne and Mandan-Hidatsa, we once again question whether the Mandan themselves manufactured the ornamented hides or secured them from others.

In 1806, the Mandan-Hidatsa took along "plenty of corn and beans to exchange with the Schians for dressed leather, robes and dried provisions. They (the Cheyenne) have a peculiar art of dressing leather which the natives of these villages have not, and this is one reason why the latter prefer it to their own. Their robes are also trimmed and garnished quite in a different manner from those of the Missourie Indians, *as they use porcupine-quills, dried straw and feathers, whilst the natives here use nothing of the kind in garnishing their robes, simply painting them black, red and blue;* so that the Schian manufacture is by far the most beautiful."[45] Thus, although in 1738 the Assiniboin purchased from the Mandan "all they could afford of such things as painted buffalo robes, skins of deer and buck, well tanned and decorated with fur and feathers . . . quill worked garters,"[46] Henry's statement causes us to wonder whether the feather and quill decoration was Mandan, while at the same time, he confirms their production of "painted" robes. Although the Mandan were very likely in contact with the Cheyenne in Verendrye's time, and some of their tales and mythology lend weight to the probability of early contact,[47] there is no definite information on where, if the Mandan did not make the ornamented robes themselves, they got them. If they did such fancy work in 1738, did they then give up the art and depend on getting it through their commercial ventures ? From the information available on the considerable amount of trade passing through the villages in the beginning of the nineteenth century, it is entirely likely that the Mandan came to rely on the equestrian nomads to provide artistically worked skins, giving up any manufacture themselves to secure them by exchange.

When, in 1802, Perrin du Lac refers to trade between the Assiniboin and Mandan, the one new item in the inventory is the horse, which the latter tribe has now secured to pass on for the European articles provided by the Assiniboin.[48]

[44] Haxo, 1941, p. 260.   [45] Henry in Coues, 1897, p. 360 (italics mine).
[46] Haxo, 1941, p. 260.
[47] Maximilian in Thwaites, 1906, Vol. 23, p. 313 ff.
[48] Perrin du Lac, op. cit., p. 63.

Nomadic and village tribes. In discussing the relations between the village tribes and the Plains nomads we shall be concerned chiefly with the Mandan, Hidatsa and Arikara on the one hand and the Cheyenne on the other; for, of all the hunting peoples of the Northern Plains during the first quarter of the nineteenth century, it appears to be the Cheyenne who had the major access to the trade of the agriculturalists.

Some idea of the potentialities of the trade among the Upper Missouri villages, especially the Mandan and Hidatsa, may be gleaned from the following statement by Mackenzie (1805), who was apparently greatly impressed with what he saw: "It is incredible the great quantity of merchandise which the Missouri Indians have accumulated by intercourse with Indians that visit them from the vicinity of commercial establishments."[49] It is well to bear in mind here that Mackenzie attributes the accumulation of wealth in European goods on the part of the village tribes to intertribal trade and not to direct trade with the Whites.

We know without question that it was in some way via the Upper Missouri area that the Cheyenne crossed the river into the Plains, and it would appear probable that as one of the most recent entrants into the area they would have better knowledge of, and means of access to, those tribes. But whatever the precise data are in that regard, the fact remains that, of all the equestrian hunters west of the Missouri mentioned in the historical literature, it is the Cheyenne who are most frequently alluded to. When other tribes, such as the Kiowa and Arapaho are referred to, it is in connection with the Cheyenne; and indeed, it would appear from the literature that it was the Cheyenne who introduced the others to the Upper Missouri tribes. Even before the arrival of Trudeau among the Arikara, in whose vicinity he met and traded with the Cheyenne, there had been White traders who mention only the Cheyenne in connection with the Upper Missouri villages. One of them had spent the entire winter of 1793—94 among them and said they were situated below the Pawnee Hoca (Arikara?) on the Missouri.[50] Now, although it is quite true that the Sioux (Dakota) were also very much in the vicinity, their connection with the sedentary tribes was of a somewhat different nature inasmuch as they did not depend upon them for their European goods, which they obtained in trade from the eastern bands of Sioux, the Yanktons and Sissetons. They will, however, be considered in another connection in the intertribal relations of the Upper Missouri trade.

Trudeau himself refers to "some French hunters who are here and who have seen much of the Cheyennes, Mandans and Gros Ventres,..."[51] He continues:

[49] Mackenzie in Masson, 1889, p. 346.   [50] Nasatir, 1927, pp. 66, 68.
[51] Trudeau, 1914, p. 456.

> On the Southwest and to the West, on the branches of a large river (which I name the river of the Cheyennes) which empties into the Missouri about three miles above the second Ricara village (of the two Arikara villages near the Grand River) are situated several nations called the Cayoguas (Kiowas), the Caminabiches (Arapahoes), the Pitapahotas (Noisy Pawnees ?), etc., all of different speech. The Cheyennes wander over the country along the river, a little below those first named... The vast country, not far from here, over which these different nations roam, abounds in beaver and otter, since they have never hunted these animals, not having had any intercourse with the White men. It would be easy by means of the Cheyennes, who are their friends, to extend our commerce with these nations and obtain from them fine furs.[52]

Thus, Trudeau considers that the Cheyenne would be the instrument for establishing relations with the other tribes, implying a priority for the former in Upper Missouri tribal relations. As a matter of fact, on July 6, 1795, a deputation of three Cheyennes arrived at the Arikara village in quest of Trudeau and they told him the above-mentioned nations were camped just beyond the Cheyenne. They expressed a desire to form an alliance with the Arikara "in order to obtain from them ammunition and knives, of which they were so much in need, but that the dread they felt, either of the Sioux or the Ricaras, who often killed them without provocation, prevented their approaching."[53] After considerable urging and persuasion by Trudeau "to form closer ties with the nations west of them and who are well supplied with horses" the Arikara finally sent back word to the Cheyenne "that the Ricaras unanimously wished to make an alliance with them, that here they would find guns, powder, knives, etc., in exchange for their horses to the Ricaras and their furs with the White men. . . ."[54]

Tableau seems to have had more extensive contact with the Cheyenne and definitely indicates that they introduced tribes from the interior plains to trade at the Arikara villages. By this time (1803—1805), ". . . they come regularly at the beginning of August to visit their old and faithful allies, the Ricaras", a somewhat different situation from that described by Trudeau. He goes on to say:

> . . . the Cheyenne nation has only a half-knowledge of the value of merchandise and prides itself, none the less, on being ignorant in this respect. This vain-glory has been conducive to my detriment in the slight trade of the Caninanbiches (Arapaho) and others who obstinately defer to its judgement. However it may be, it is certain that, if it had not been for the interference of the Cheyennes, I should have made better use of the nations who accompanied them this year for the first time in their visit to the Ricaras.[55]

Not only that, but the Arikara the year before accompanied the Cheyenne to a rendezvous in the Black Hills where they traded corn and

---

[52] *Ibid.*, p. 461.
[54] *Ibid.*, pp. 467, 468.
[53] *Ibid.*, p. 466.
[55] Tabeau in Abel, 1939, p. 153.

tobacco to "eight other friendly nations – the Caninanbiches (Arapaho),
the Squihitanes (Snake ?, Sissetons ?), the Nimoussines, the Padaucas,
the Catarkas (all three Comanches ?), the Datamis (Kiowa ?, Comanche ?),
the Tchiwak (Chaui ?) and the Cayawa (Kiowa)."[56]

Nomadic and forest tribes. Reference was made in a previous chapter to
the account of the destruction of the Sheyenne-Cheyenne site which
Thompson obtained from the Chippewa chief, Sheshepaskut. If we
accept the date of that incident as approximately 1770, then the story is
not only interesting for the fact that the Cheyenne already had horses
while practicing agriculture in addition to buffalo hunting, but also for
the evidence it contains of the existence of trade relations and an uneasy
peace between the Cheyenne and the Chippewa. Although no mention is
made of the type of goods the Cheyenne received in the exchange, it is
clear that the Chippewa were interested in their horticultural produce.
As the Chippewa chief said to Thompson, "Our people and the Cheyennes for several years had been doubtful friends; but as they had Corn
and other Vegetables, which we had not and of which we were fond, and
traded with them, we passed over and forgot, many things we did not
like; ... some of our people went to trade corn; ..."[57]

Thus, we see that by about the third quarter of the eighteenth
century the Cheyenne were engaged in trade with tribes to the northeast. And since the latter were in an area of extensive trade with
Europeans, it is almost certain that the Cheyenne were in possession of
articles of European manufacture through the intertribal trade. The
archaeological evidence, though meagre, indicates that some material
at least found its way to the Sheyenne-Cheyenne site where the excavations revealed the presence of blue and white trade beads (the latter
inserted in pottery), brass and copper danglers, a fragment of glass,
brass and iron arrow and lance points, metal knife-like objects, a
probable gunflint, miscellaneous pieces of metal, and a brass piece of the
ornamental forward extension of a trigger guard. The latter object
resembles those found on British guns made about 1710, or it may
possibly be from a gun of French make of about 1700.[58]

Types of Goods Exchanged

In the trade which took place at the Upper Missouri villages between
the Plains nomads and the horticultural tribes, the nomads exchanged
horses and mules, dried meat, fat, prairie-turnip flour, dressed skins,
leather "tents," buffalo robes, furs, shirts and leggings of deer and

---

[56] *Ibid.*, p. 154.   [57] Thompson in Tyrrell, 1916, p. 261.
[58] Strong, 1940, p. 373. References to the use of these beads are also made by
Lewis and Clark in Thwaites, 1904, Vol. 5. pp. 356—357; and by Tabeau in
Abel, 1939, pp. 171, 176.

antelope skin ornamented with quill work, moccasins, etc. The village tribes supplied corn, beans, melons, pumpkins, tobacco, and other plants, guns, powder, bullets, kettles, axes, knives, awls, beads, mirrors, etc.

In general, the classes of objects produced by the nomads were animal: furs, food, and native clothing. Those "produced" by the horticulturalists were food and European articles. The most important articles in the exchange were firearms and horses, the value of each being set in terms of the other, though the worth of other goods should not be underestimated. The Arikara, for example, were extremely fond of prairie-turnip flour and gave three or four measures of corn for one of the flour.[59] However, a horse would ordinarily be paid for "with a gun, a hundred charges of powder and balls, a knife and other trifles."[60] In the unsuccessful peace meeting in 1806 between the Cheyenne and the Hidatsa, it was tacitly understood beforehand, and finally made explicit by one of the Hidatsa chiefs, that his tribe "were ready to give good guns and ammunition, but expected to receive good horses in return."[61] La Rocque, among the Mandan in 1804, "bought a stout mule for which I paid: 1 gun, 1 large axe, 1 awl, 1 looking glass, 1 fathom Hudson's Bay red strouds, 1 fathom tobacco, 2 flints, 3 strings pipe beads, 300 balls and powder, 2 knives, 2 wormers, and a little vermillion."[62] It will be remembered that in Bradbury's description of the trade at the Arikara in 1810, Hunt had to give in exchange for horses, "carbines, powder, ball, tomahawks, knives, etc."[63]

On the other hand, the remaining trade of the Indians was conducted entirely in terms of native production. When Lewis and Clark stopped at an Arikara village on their return trip, they met a trading camp of Cheyenne "who have come to trade with the Rickarees for corn and beans, for which they give in exchange buffaloe meat and robes."[64] On the Hidatsa peace expedition to the Cheyenne, the women were told to take along "plenty of corn and beans, to exchange with the Schians for dressed leather, robes and dried provisions."[65] As Tabeau points out "The Cheyennes having themselves been farmers put a higher value on the (horticultural) commodities and, with more difficulty, go without them."[66] It would, therefore, appear that "production" of horses among the Plains nomads was strictly for trade in European goods, whereas aboriginal goods were traded on a separate basis. Tabeau, after pointing out that horses are exchanged for guns between the Cheyenne and Arikara, implies that there was a separate exchange in native articles when he writes: "Deer leather, well-dressed shirts of antelope-skin, ornamented and worked with different-colored quills of the porcupine,

[59] Tabeau in Abel, 1939, p. 98.
[60] Ibid., p. 158.
[61] Henry in Coues, 1897, p. 389.
[62] La Rocque in Masson, 1889, p. 308.
[63] Bradbury in Thwaites, 1906, p. 132,
[64] Gass in Hosmer, 1904, p. 278.
[65] Henry in Coues, 1897, p. 360.
[66] Tabeau in Abel, 1939, p. 151.

shoes, and especially a quantity of dried meat and of prairie-apple flour are traded for certain commodities, particularly for the tobacco, which the Ricaras sell to them very well, because of this value."[67]

From the evidence it would also appear that whereas both sexes engaged in trade, each exchanged the goods with which they were most concerned. This is clearly seen in Henry's description of the trading which took place in the Cheyenne camp, where women were involved in exchanging native goods, while the men were concerned among themselves with horses and firearms.

Mackenzie, interestingly enough, ties up the right of sanctuary for strangers in Hidatsa villages with the commercial proclivities of the inhabitants. Although the foreigners often killed their benefactors and made off with their scalps, the Hidatsa apparently felt that the commercial game was worth the candle. For, as Mackenzie writes, "Though the Enasas are sensible to this treachery from dire experience, they still encourage the perpetual presence of strangers, for they sometimes find it convenient to make use of them as interpreters to traffic with the many Indians who resort to that quarter in the summer season, and, sometimes, as ambassadors to distant nations, for arrangements of differences."[68]

Some Trade Patterns

Although descriptions in the historical literature of actual trading are very few, and those incomplete, it is probably safe to say that there were two general patterns in the trade relations between the Plains nomads and the village tribes – ceremonial tribal trade and individual trade. Probably the best account of the former is given by Mackenzie who witnessed, at a Hidatsa village in 1805, the spectacular arrival of three hundred tents of Crow Indians who had with them over two thousand horses. After giving a remarkable demonstration of superlative horsemanship in charging down into and through the village, the Crow had the "compliment" returned to them the following day by the Hidatsa who, dressed in all their finery, gave a similar exhibition. "These, having the advantage of residing in the vicinity of trading establishments, were better provided with necessaries and consequently had a more warlike appearance, but they were inferior in the management of their horses."[69] However, the actual trade began the following day:

Les Gros Ventres made the (Crow) . . . smoke the pipe of friendship, and, at the same time, laid before them a present consisting of two hundred guns, with one hundred rounds of ammunition for each, a hundred bushels of Indian corn, a certain quantity of mercantile articles, such as kettles, axes, clothes, etc. The (Crow) in return brought two hundred and fifty horses, large

[67] *Ibid.*, p. 158.   [68] Mackenzie in Masson, 1889, p. 360.   [69] *Ibid.*, p. 345.

parcels of (buffaloe) robes, leather leggins, shirts, etc., etc. This exchange of trading civilities took place dancing; when the dancing was over, the presents were distributed among the individuals in proportion to the value of the articles respectively furnished; this dance therefore is a rule of traffic. The Mandane villages exchanged similar civilities with the same tribe.[70]

If the Crow exchanged a like amount of goods with the Mandan, then the total of the transactions for the Crow was very considerable.

This method of tribal exchange is called trading "on the pipe." Although the same method is described by Mackenzie and Henry for the Cheyenne and Hidatsa ceremonial trade, that affair was complicated by the ceremonies of adoption the purpose of which was to cement a peace between the tribes. That the primary purpose of the peace making was to establish friendly trade relations, there seems to be little doubt. Le Borgne, the Hidatsa chief, told Mackenzie, "My son," said he, "to-morrow I am to adopt one of the Shawyens for my son, and am to offer them a 'pipe' on which the Gros Ventres will put all their goods and the Shawyens their horses. *According to our manner of trade* we ought to expect at least two hundred horses as we have that number of guns, besides other articles, to put on the Pipe."[71] Le Borgne knew well his reasons for desiring peace with the Cheyenne, who, according to Henry, had "the best built and most active horses I had seen in this country – superior in every respect, to those we see to the northward."[72]

Unfortunately, neither the peace nor the trade was concluded because of the appearance of twelve Assiniboin whom the Cheyenne wished to kill, but who were taken under protection by the Hidatsa. The latter were more numerous and far better armed, as the Assiniboin knew before they appeared upon the scene. Though attempts were made by the Hidatsa to go on with the peace and trade, the Cheyennes were in a sullen, sulking mood and only made grudging and feeble gestures to accomplish the purpose of the meeting. Had everything gone as originally planned, the trade might have been concluded in the expeditious manner of the Crow-Hidatsa ceremonial trade described by Mackenzie. As it turns out, we have instead what may be termed a bargaining process, because of the obvious aversion of the Cheyenne toward the proceedings. Nevertheless, it is clear that as each side brought forward objects for the exchange it was placed under or near the "pipe" around which the proceedings took place.

The Big Bellies brought in some ammunition and laid it upon the strouds; the son (adopted by Le Borgne, the Hidatsa chief) was directed to lay the stem (pipe) over these articles, which he did accordingly. Our old general was again posted opposite the entrance of the shelter, where he was fully employed in his usual vocation of haranguing, inviting everyone to put something under

[70] *Ibid.*, p. 346.   [72] Henry in Coues, 1897, p. 377.
[71] *Ibid.*, p. 387 (italics mine).

the stem. But all his eloquence was in vain; not a Schian came forward until some of their old men had gone the rounds making long speeches, when a few of the Schians appeared with some garnished robes and dressed leather, which were spread on the ground near the bull's head, which was then laid upon the heap. The Big Bellies next brought two guns, which they placed under the stem. The Schians put another robe or two under the bull's head. Our party were each time more ready to come forward with their property than the others were with theirs. The latter next brought some old, scabby, sore-backed horses for the bull's head. This compliment was returned by our party with corn, beans, ammunition and a gun. General Chokecherry grew impatient, and reproached the Schians in a very severe and harsh manner for their mean and avaricious manner of dealing, in bringing forward their trash and rotten horses, *saying that the Big Bellies were ready to give good guns and ammunition, but expected to receive good horses in return.* In answer to this they were given to understand by the Schians that they must first put all their guns and ammunition under the stem, immediately after which the Schians, in their turn, would bring in good horses. As it was never customary in an affair of this kind for either party to particularize the articles to be brought to the stem or bull's head, but for everyone to contribute what he pleased of the best he had, this proposal induced our party to suspect the Schians had planned to get our firearms and ammunition into their possession, that they might be a match for us, and commence hostilities. To prevent this, no more guns or ammunition were brought forward, and the Schians were told they must first produce some of their best horses; but to this they would not listen. After a few more trifles had been given in on both sides, the business came to a standstill on the part of the Schians, who retired to their tents.[73]

The manner of individual trade is again briefly described by Henry, and it is apparently conducted by the women. "The (Hidatsa) women were also busy exchanging their corn for leather, robes, smocks, and dried provisions, as if at a country fair. Each one was anxious to dispose of her property to advantage, and to this end carried a load from tent to tent. But the numerous women of our party had overstocked the market, and many were obliged to keep half of what they had brought for want of buyers."[74] Earlier the principal men of the Cheyenne had harangued the people, urging them among other things to "exchange their own commodities upon equal terms..."[75]

The foregoing situation produced by the presence of the few Assiniboins in the midst of intended peace and trade proceedings, is worth examining more closely for the implications it contains with regard to intertribal relations against the background of trade. It is quite clear, as we have already seen, that the Assiniboin and Hidatsa had been engaged in trade for many years, at least as far back as 1738, and undoubtedly earlier. The former tribe, being in direct contact with British and/or French traders, was one of the chief sources of European goods for the Hidatsa. It was, therefore, basic diplomacy for them not to alienate such an important source of income. Indeed, such a policy was

[73] *Ibid.*, pp. 390—391 (italics mine).
[74] *Ibid.*, pp. 384—385.   [75] *Ibid.*, p. 380.

specifically articulated in another situation by an Arikara before a council, attended by Lewis and Clark, with the Mandan in which he defended the friendship of his tribe with the Sioux. Addressing the Mandan chiefs, he said:

> ... you know that the Ricarees are Dependant on the Seeaux for their guns, powder and Ball, and it was policy in them to keep on as good tirms as possible with the Seaux untill they had Some other means of getting those articles Ec. Ec. You know yourselves that you are compelled to put up with little insults from the Christinoes (Cree), Ossinaboins (or Stone Inds,) because if you go to war with those people, they will provent the traders in the North from bringing you Guns, Powder and Ball and by that means distress you very much.[76]

In view of such an attitude it is not difficult to understand the solicitude of the Hidatsa for the Assiniboins who, apparently, were long time enemies of the Cheyenne.[77] The original intention of the peacemaking, the initiative for which came from the Cheyenne, was undoubtedly the establishment of friendly trade relations. Though the Cheyenne were more often engaged in trade with the Arikara, the Sioux had for some years been creating difficulties in the relations of other groups with the Arikara. Since it was also apparent that the Mandan and Hidatsa had access to many sources, native and White, of European goods, the Cheyenne probably attempted to open another avenue for the acquisition of those articles; and to make it more secure, they returned a prisoner to the Hidatsa and offered one of their young men to Le Borgne, the Hidatsa chief, for adoption as a son. Just as in numerous instances a trade situation between people is not phrased in the "uncouth" parlance of commerce, but as friendly gift giving, so the word "trade" was never once mentioned by either side in the peace preliminaries at the Hidatsa village. But among themselves it was another matter. The Hidatsa women, as we saw, were told to take plenty of corn and beans to trade. The men brought guns, ammunition, European goods; numerous horses were loaded. Each time the Cheyenne trip was mentioned to Mackenzie by Le Borgne, he spoke of it in terms of trade, especially for horses.[78]

Trudeau writes that "... among all savage people the most wise words and discourses, whether for peace, whether for war, or in regard to the reception of strangers, are not fruitful, if unaccompanied by feasts and by presents of horses, guns or other merchandise given at the end."[79] According to Tabeau "The horse is the most important article of their (the Cheyenne) trade with the Ricaras. Most frequently it is given as a present; but, according to their manner, that is to say, is recalled when

---

[76] Lewis and Clark in Thwaites, 1904, Vol. I, p. 231 (original orthography).
[77] Grinnell, 1923b, Vol. I, p. 23; Will, 1913—14, pp. 71—72.
[78] Mackenzie in Masson, 1889, pp. 382 and 387.
[79] Trudeau, 1914, p. 470.

the tender in exchange does not please. This is an understood restriction. This present is paid ordinarily with a gun, a hundred charges of powder and balls, a knife and other trifles."[80]

Although gift exchange is an old and widespread pattern for cementing social solidarity both in intertribal and intra-tribal affairs, with the increased importance of trade in the lives of people and their dependence upon the objects secured in that trade, the question arises as to whether the relation between cause and effect has not undergone a change. It is not difficult to see that the desire to obtain the benefits of trade would induce a group to seek establishment of a formal peace with another group which is in a position to supply trade goods. Yet the exchange may still be phrased in terms of gift giving for the *apparently* primary purpose of making peace. The important aspect of the actual situations described here is that the "gifts" are by no means symbolic, but are objects upon which the highest value is placed because they are so important in the life of the people.

[80] Tabeau in Abel, 1939, p. 158.

CHAPTER THREE

EFFECTS ON PLAINS TRIBAL RELATIONS

Tribal Antagonisms

Although Lewis and Clark state that the Cheyenne, Arapaho, Kiowa and other western tribes occasionally came to the Mandan for purposes of trade, it is with the Arikara that the Cheyenne are mentioned in the literature as being most often engaged in commerce. This is true at least until 1811 or 1813, and probably later. But the western bands of the Dakota, who, from the latter part of the eighteenth century on, were the bane of the Upper Missouri tribes because of their plundering raids, had a special affinity for the Arikara, whom they attempted to keep under their constant domination. This was a considerable source of annoyance to the Cheyenne, and, as indicated above, probably prompted them to seek additional avenues of trade through a more permanent peace with the Hidatsa and Mandan. Until that time, relations between the latter tribes and the Cheyenne were rather tenuous and suspicious, because of the friendship of the Cheyenne with the Arikara, who often assisted the Dakota in their depredations against the Mandan-Hidatsa villages. Furthermore, the Arikara were competitors of the Mandan-Hidatsa in that they invariably attempted to prevent traders coming up the Missouri from St. Louis from proceeding further to the former tribes. In addition, it was to the Arikara that the Cheyenne brought the trade of the other nomadic Plains tribes. The relations of the Cheyenne and the Sioux were also of a very tenuous nature, as the latter resented their trading with the Arikara for objects they themselves (the Sioux) could supply. However, the Mandan-Hidatsa assumed friendly relations to exist between the Cheyenne and Sioux also. Thus, when during the visit of Lewis and Clark among the Mandan in 1804, "Six Chiens . . . arrived with a pipe and said that their nation was at one days march and intended to come and trade Ec. . . . The Mandans apprehended danger from the Sharhas (Cheyenne) as they were at peace with the Sioux; and wished to kill them and the (three Arikaras who accompanied the Cheyenne)."[1] While one of the important purposes of Lewis and Clark was to establish peace among the tribes they met in their explorations, the existence of such a complicated competitive situation for which the Sioux were really basically responsible, was hardly conducive to the success of the explorers' good intentions. It is interesting to note in this

[1] Lewis and Clark in Thwaites, 1904, Vol. I, p. 232.

connection that the unsuccessful peace meeting between the Cheyenne and Hidatsa took place on July 25, 1806.[2] The following August 15, when Lewis and Clark were among the Hidatsa, "... the great chief of the Menetaras (Hidatsa) ... said ... he had made peace with the Cheyennes...", but that, "... the Ricaras had stolen from his people a number of horses at different times and his people had killed 2 Ricaras ... they were all afraid of the Sieoux..."[3] This misrepresentation by the chief of the true state of affairs between his tribe and the Cheyenne was undoubtedly made to maintain his friendship with the Whites whenever possible. They were, after all, the source of supply of European goods.

Sioux and Arikara Relations

Ever since the western bands of the Dakota reached the Missouri, they were the scourge of the Mandan, Hidatsa and Arikara villages. Trudeau wrote that they "are enemies of the Mandans, the Gros Ventres and the Ricaras, and other nations also."[4] "The Sioux nations are feared and dreaded by all of these others on account of the fire arms with which they are always well provided; their very name causes terror, they having so often ravaged and carried off the wives and children of the Ricaras."[5] Lewis and Clark write not only of their "piratical aggressions," their "distressing and plundering the traders of the Missouri, but also plundering and massacreing the defenceless savages of the Missouri, from the mouth of the river Platte to the Minetares (Hidatsa), and west to the Rocky Mountains."[6] Perrin Du Lac wrote of the Sioux, "This people, who are deceitful and cruel, often plunder the Ricaras and Chaguyennes of clothes and horses, and the Mandans of maize and tobacco."[7]

Nevertheless, the peculiar subordination of the Arikara to the Sioux is a fact commented upon in a number of journals since the time of Trudeau. Le Raye, who was among the Arikara in 1802, added a little more to the picture when he wrote: "... the Sioux ... have got them so far under subjection, that they dare not offend them, and are frequently robbed, plundered, and even murdered, without daring to resent it. This information was given me by an old chief of the lower villages."[8] It is

[2] Henry in Coues, 1897, p. 388.
[3] Lewis and Clark in Thwaites, 1904, Vol. V, p. 340.
[4] Trudeau, 1914, p. 63.
[5] *Ibid.*, p. 455.
[6] Lewis and Clark in Thwaites, 1904, Vol. VI, p. 96.
[7] Perrin Du Lac, 1807, p. 63.
[8] Le Raye, in Cutler, 1812, p. 174. While Le Raye is generally considered a dubious source, his statements as quoted here, are amply borne out by contemporary writers who refer to the identical situation which we are here considering.

Tabeau, however, who provides a detailed account of the nature of the relationship in which the Arikara seem to be completely at the mercy of the Sioux who dictate the terms, whether it be trade, provision of food, or robbery.

> ... in the Ricaras (the Sioux have) a certain kind of serf, who cultivate for them and who, as they say, takes, for them, the place of women... they live together always in a state of war and mutual distrust. The Ricaras cannot let their horses out of sight and are compelled at night to tie them to their lodges... Around the end of August the Sioux come from all parts loaded with dried meat, with fat, with dressed leather, and some merchandise. They fix, as they wish, the price of that which belongs to them and obtain, in exchange, a quantity of corn, tobacco, beans and pumpkins that they demand. They camp then near by on the plains, which they openly pillage without anyone opposing them except by complaints and feeble reproaches. They steal the horses and they beat the women and offer with impunity all kinds of insults.
>
> Well provided with commodities they wander for some time far from the village, while surrounding it and forming a barrier which prevents the buffalo from coming near. From there they still bring from time to time loads of meat and undressed skins which constitute the largest part of the robes which the Ricaras furnish...[9]

It would appear that we have here in microcosm a case in which there exist some of the elements of colonial exploitation. This situation was seen in substantially the same light by Lewis and Clark, who said that the Arikara

> ... claim no land except that on which their villages stand and the fields which they cultivate. The Tetons claim the country around them. Though they are the oldest inhabitants, they may be properly considered the farmers or tenants at will of that lawless, savage and rapacious race the Sioux Teton, who rob them of their horses, plunder their gardens and fields, and sometimes murder them, without opposition. If these people were freed from the oppression of the Tetons, their trade would increase rapidly... They maintain a partial trade with their oppressors the Tetons, to whom they barter horses, mules, corn, beans, and a species of tobacco which they cultivate; and receive in return guns, ammunition, kettles, axes, and other articles which the Tetons obtain from the Yanktons of N. and Sissatones, who trade with Mr. Cammeron, on the river St. Peters. These horses and mules the Ricaras obtain from their western neighbors, who visit them frequently for the purpose of trafficking.[10]

Tabeau succinctly contrasts the relationship of the Arikara with the Sioux on the one hand and with the Cheyenne on the other in stating: "The commodities of the Ricaras attract almost all the year a large crowd of Sioux from whom the Ricaras have to endure much without deriving any real benefit. It is not so with the Cheyennes and many other wandering nations, whom they supply with maize, tobacco, beans,

[9] Tabeau in Abel, 1939, pp. 130—131.
[10] Lewis and Clark in Thwaites, 1904, Vol. VI, p. 89.

pumpkins, etc. These people visit them as true friends and the advantages of the trade is almost equal. The Cheyennes, having themselves been farmers, put a highesvalue on the commodities and with more difficulty go without them."[11]

In the face of the oppression and depredations they suffered at the hands of the Sioux, we nevertheless find the Arikara defending their relationship with them. For in spite of the fact that the advantage of the exchange obviously rested with the Sioux, the Arikara still considered the latter to be their most important source of European trade goods, especially guns. Although they did have access at various times to the direct trade of the Whites who came among them, they were in this respect somewhat in the situation of being between Scylla and Charybdis. In the north the Mandan and Hidatsa formed a barrier to their trade with the Canadians, while to the south the traders from St. Louis had not only to pass the tribes situated on the lower reaches of the Missouri, but also to get by the Sioux, who were ever on the alert to see that the Arikara and the tribes beyond were not supplied from this source. Therefore, in spite of the hatred the Arikara bore the Sioux, we saw above how in November of 1804, in council with Lewis and Clark and the Mandan, the Arikara specifically stated that they were dependent upon the Sioux for their guns and ammunition, and that until they had access to such goods from another source, they had to maintain their connections with the Sioux. When in August, 1806, Lewis and Clark again admonished the Arikara for maintaining their ties with the Sioux, "(the chiefs) promised to attend strictly to what had been Said to them, and observed that they must trade with the Sieoux one more time to get guns and powder; that they had no guns or powder and had more horses than they had use for, after they got guns and powder that they would never again have anything to do with them etc. etc..."[12] Even had the Arikara sincerely desired to terminate their relationship with the Sioux it is highly doubtful if their situation would have permitted it.

Inasmuch as the western bands of the Dakota supplied the Arikara with guns and European goods, it is clear that the former were not dependent on the Missouri trade for those articles. Their source of supply lay in the eastern bands of Dakota who traded with the British on the upper reaches of the Mississippi, especially along the Minnesota River. In order to engage in this trade they had to supply the Sisseton and Yankton Sioux with goods of native production, and their domination over the Arikara helped them to increase the amount of native goods they were able to supply for this trade.

As early as 1795, Trudeau records that the western Sioux were feared on the Missouri "on account of the fire arms with which they are always

[11] Tabeau in Abel, 1939, p. 151.
[12] Lewis and Clark in Thwaites, 1904, Vol. V, p. 356.

well provided;..."[13] and they possessed these guns because "It is their custom every spring to meet the other Sioux villages, situated on the St. Pierre (Minnesota) and Des Moines rivers, with whom they trade the r furs for merchandise."[14] In 1803, Le Raye accompanied a band of Tetons to meet Yanktons and other Sioux on the Minnesota for purposes of trading.[15] Tabeau writes that the Tetons:

> ... by different routes upon the east bank (of the Missouri) go into the heart of the prairies to a kind of market, where are found also every spring the Yinctons of the North and of the South, the Scissitons, some people of the Leaves and often even some of the Lakes.[16] This concourse is sometimes composed of a thousand to twelve hundred lodges, about three thousand men bearing arms. Much trading is done there. Each man brings different articles, according to the places over which he has wandered. Those who have frequented the St. Peter's River and that of the Mohens furnish guns, kettles, red pipes, and bows of walnut. The Titons give in exchange horses, lodges of leather, buffalo robes, shirts and leggings of antelope-skin.[17]

Lewis and Clark further clarify the nature of the trade relations existing between the eastern and western Dakota and show how it placed the Teton in a position which enabled them to have an independent source of supply of guns and other goods, and thereby exploit the Arikara and practice hostilities against other tribes and White traders. Because the Arikara apparently had a sufficiently large population which could provide them with necessary commodities on their own terms, the Sioux could engage in indiscriminate raiding up and down the Missouri without in any way jeopardizing any possible source of trade income to themselves. There were no other tribes on the Upper Missouri or in the Interior Plains which could afford to indulge in wholesale plunder like the Sioux without cutting themselves off from the trade relations of the Missouri. The Sioux, not requiring the Missouri trade as a legitimate source of income could indulge themselves in the luxury of plunder, the only cost to them being that of making enemies.

> The Sioux annually hold a fair on some part of the (James) river, in the latter end of May. thither the Yanktons of the North, and the Sissitons, who trade with a Mr. Cammaron on the head of the St. Peters river, bring guns, pouder & balls, kettles, axes, knives, and a variety of European manufactures, which they barter to the 4 bands of Tetons and the Yanktons Ahnah, who inhabit the borders of the Missouri and upper part of the River Demoin, and receive in exchange horses, leather lodges and buffaloe robes, which they have either manufactured or plundered from other Indian nations on the Missouri and west of it. This traffic is sufficient to keep the Sioux of the Missouri tolerably well supplied with arms and ammunition, thus rendering them independent of the trade of the Missouri and enableing them to continue their piratical aggressions on all who attempt to ascent that river, as well as to disturb perpetually the tranquility of all their Indian neighbors.[18]

[13] Trudeau, 1914, p. 455.   [14] *Ibid.*, p. 474.
[15] Le Raye in Cutler, 1812, p. 201.   [16] These are all Sioux bands.
[17] Tabeau in Abel, 1939, pp. 121—122.
[18] Lewis and Clark in Thwaites, 1904, Vol. VI, p. 45.

... (Sisseton) country abounds more in the valuable fur animals, the beaver, otter and marten, than any portion of Louisiana yet known. This circumstance furnishes the Sissatones with the means of purchasing more merchandise in proportion to their number, than any nation in this quarter. A great proportion of this merchandise is reserved by them for their trade with the Tetons, whom they annually meet at some point previously agreed on, upon the waters of James river, in the month of May. This Indian fair is frequently attended by the Yanktons of the North and Ahnah. The Sissatones and Yanktons of the North here supply the others with considerable quantities of arms, ammunition, axes, knives, kettles, cloth, and a variety of other articles; and receive in return principally horses, which the others have stolen or purchased from the nations on the Missouri and west of it. They are devoted to the interests of their traders.[19]

The Cheyenne in the Sioux-Arikara Situation

In their attempt to monopolize the production of the Arikara, the Teton Dakota came into opposition with the nomadic tribes west of the Missouri, especially the Cheyenne. Trudeau, while among the Arikara, mentions trying to "maintain peace with the Cheyennes and the village of the Sioux settled here, who are at variance with one another."[20] Le Raye who arrived at the mouth of the Cheyenne River on April 14, 1802, wrote that "... On the head waters reside several tribes of Indians, with which the Sioux are at war, the most powerful of these tribes are the Chien, or Dog Indians."[21]

Tabeau also stated that the Cheyenne and Sioux "live in mutual fear of treachery and always, potentially, in a state of war. At their meeting with the Ricaras, the Missouri separated the two camps, and, as the Chayennes occupied the bank where the Ricara villages are, the jealous Sioux wished to cross in order to camp near them. The Chayennes opposed this with firmness and with threats and the Sioux manifested neither obstinacy nor offense. They contented themselves with saying to the Ricaras that they would be avenged for this noticeable favor."[22] Lewis and Clark write that the Cheyenne "... confess to be at war with no nation except the Sieoux..."[23]

Now, although the hostility between the Cheyenne and Sioux has a long history behind it, probably dating from the time they were neighbors in Minnesota, it would appear that trade situations, especially with the Arikara involved, invariably aggravated this antagonism. Both the Sioux and the Cheyenne desired the crops raised by the Arikara, but the Sioux set their own price. Both the Cheyenne and Sioux brought dried meat, fat, dressed leather. Thus, similar products could be supplied to the Arikara by these two tribes: whereas their great differences lay in

[19] *Ibid.*, p. 95.   [20] Trudeau, 1914, p. 470.
[21] Le Raye in Cutler, 1812, p. 171.   [22] Tabeau in Abel, 1939, p. 152.
[23] Lewis and Clark in Thwaites, 1904, Vol. V, p. 357.

the fact that the Cheyenne brought horses and the Sioux brought guns and European goods. Thus, although the Sioux and Cheyenne had the most important exchangeable commodities which normally would not have to pass through the Arikara middlemen, those two tribes never entered into direct trade negotiations during this period. Apart from historical enmity, which rarely is permitted to stand in the way of mutual advantages to be derived from certain situations, particularly trade, there were some practical and cogent reasons as to why the Sioux should have resented the presence of the Cheyenne and others among the Arikara. In the first place, the Sioux did not like to see their guns passed on to the Cheyenne, for in order for the Arikara to obtain horses from the Cheyenne, they had to trade guns, powder and ball. Secondly, the Sioux desired to exploit the Arikara for their own benefit in their own way, and it was not part of their objective to encourage trade on the Missouri. On the contrary, their whole purpose was to disrupt the Missouri trade as far as possible, and in a certain sense they used the Arikara as a base of operations. The Sioux encouraged the Arikara to secure their horses not through trade, but through robbery, and to this end often compelled them to join them in raiding the Mandan and Hidatsa. In this way, the Sioux could also secure horses from the Arikara pretty much on their own terms, either by stealing them in turn from the Arikara, or purchasing them if they had to. As we saw above, in the exchange between the Teton and Sisseton and Yankton, the horse was the most important article. But if, in order to get more horses for this trade, the Tetons had to trade the guns which they originally obtained for horses, they did not gain thereby. It was therefore their special relationship with the Arikara, and also their raiding, which permitted them to make the margin of profit necessary to give them a dominant position.

In view of such a rationale as the Sioux possessed, they could not regard with favor any trade between the Arikara and Cheyenne. However, the Sioux were far from being able to carry out their intentions on the Missouri to their complete satisfaction. Too often, perhaps, they had to stand by and watch numerous Cheyenne, Arapaho, Kiowa, Comanche and others trading at the Arikara villages.[24] It may be said, though, that the Sioux and the Cheyenne found themselves in the position of competing for certain advantages to be derived from the trade of the Arikara. While the latter were equal trade partners with the Cheyenne, they were, on the other hand, to a large extent, vassals of the Sioux. It was apparently impossible for the vassals to function as free agents without arousing resentment in the hearts of the masters against the parties treating them as free agents. And so, the earlier antagonism between Cheyenne and Sioux was nursed and kept warm by the exigencies of trade.

[24] Tabeau in Abel, 1939, p. 162; Le Raye in Cutler, 1812, pp. 173—174.

According to the account contained in Luttig's Journal for the winter of 1812—13, the only tribes camped in the vicinity of Fort Manuel in South Dakota were Cheyenne, Arikara and Sioux. The Cheyenne and Arikara, particularly the former, were trading at the post for their furs, meat, moccasins, tongues, etc., while the Arikara were securing meat from the Cheyenne. The Sioux had nothing to trade but meat, but their major purpose was obviously to create trouble with the other two tribes, and also with the Whites. Whereas the Cheyenne and Arikara were on friendly terms, the Sioux soon began hostilities by killing an Arikara; and Luttig implies that a few nights later they fought with the Cheyenne. The following month the Sioux attacked the fort itself, unsuccessfully, and wound up their stay by stealing twenty-four horses from the Cheyenne.[25]

This account is cited merely to indicate the continuing pattern of the relations, during the first quarter of the nineteenth century, between the Sioux on the one hand, and the Cheyenne, Arikara and Whites on the other. West of the Missouri, during the period when the western Dakota had a reliable source of trade goods from the British via their eastern relatives, they had at no time friendly trade relations with any of the tribes. They pursued a path of war and conquest to acquire the commodities necessary for their own trade. Indirectly, they too, like the Sisseton and Yankton were "devoted to the interests of their (British) traders" on the upper Mississippi, and were attempting to disrupt the developing trade of the Americans.

The Cheyenne as Middlemen

We have seen earlier that the Cheyenne, probably because of their horticultural background and the fact that during the period of their equestrian nomadism they were entering the Great Plains in the vicinity of the Upper Missouri villages, had a certain priority (among the nomads) in the trade of the horticulturalists. It was through the Cheyenne that the White traders learned of the tribes beyond; it was they who came alone or with others to the villages. In a conclave of tribes at the villages, one or another of the nomads may not have been present at any one time, but the Cheyenne seem always to have been mentioned. And it was the Cheyenne who between 1803 and 1805, brought the Arikara on a trading expedition to a rendezvous with other tribes in the Black Hills.

In addition to the intertribal trade which took place at the Upper Missouri villages, there developed also a regular trade among the equestrian nomads of the Interior Plains at certain designated places. It was in this trade that the Cheyenne apparently assumed one of the major roles as middlemen between the villages and other nomadic tribes.

[25] Luttig, 1920, pp. 108—127.

In this situation, the exchange was limited and specific with respect to the commodities employed in the transaction, the Cheyenne bringing European goods which were bartered only for horses. Inasmuch as all these tribes produced substantially similar native goods, the exchange of such articles was relatively limited, though it occurred. Bradbury, during the period 1809—1811, saw at an Arikara village, a Cheyenne who "was covered with a buffalo robe, curiously ornamented with figures worked with split quills, stained red and yellow, intermixed with much taste, and the border of the robe entirely hung round with the hoofs of young fawns, which at every moment made a noise much resembling that of the rattlesnake when that animal is irritated. I understood that this robe had been purchased from the Arapahoes..."[26]

What seems to be the earliest reference to the function of the Cheyenne as middlemen for other nomadic Plains tribes is contained in James' account of Long's Expedition. When, in July, 1820, the party was in the vicinity of Denver, near Cherry Creek, a tributary of the South Platte, he wrote that:

> About four years previous (approximately 1816) to the time of our visit, there had been a large encampment of Indians and hunters on this creek. On that occasion, three nations of Indians, namely, the Kiowas, Arrapahoes, and Kaskaias, or Badhearts (?), had been assembled together, with forty-five French hunters in the employ of Mr. Choteau and Mr. Demun of St. Louis. They had assembled for the purpose of holding a trading council with a band of Shiennes. These last had been recently supplied with goods by the British traders on the Missouri, and had come to exchange them with the former for horses. The Kiawas, Arrapahoes, etc. who wander in the fertile plains of the Arkansa and Red river, have always great numbers of horses, which they rear with much less difficulty than the Shiennes, whose country is cold and barren.[27]

We thus learn also that while the Cheyenne are still living in the north, the Arapaho and Kiowa are well established in the Southern Plains near the more abundant supply of horses which they are trading to the Cheyenne. In a later passage, James clearly indicates how the flow of goods from the Upper Missouri is maintained among the tribes in its passage to the Interior Plains groups. He writes:

> The British traders annually supply the Minnetarees or Gros Ventres of the Missouri with goods; from these they pass to the Shiennes and Crow Indians, who, in their turn, barter them with remoter tribes: in this manner the Indians who wander near the mountains receive their supplies of goods, and they give a decided and well founded preference to those which reach them by this circuitous channel, to those which they receive from any other source.[28]

[26] Bradbury in Thwaites, 1906, p. 139.
[27] James in Thwaites, 1906, Vol. XV, p. 282.
[28] *Ibid*, pp. 284—285.

In this latter connection, it would appear that often the interior tribes felt more secure in their business dealings with other Indians than they did with the Whites. It was mentioned previously how, to the despair of Tabeau, the Arapaho deferred to the judgment of the Cheyenne when the former tribe came to trade with Tabeau. Mackenzie, who, in 1805, tried to trade with the Crow during their trading visit among the Hidatsa and Mandan, said of them, "Afraid to ask too small a price, they seemed averse from dealing with me, for they would have a white man pay four times the value of a thing, or often let him go without."[29]

James also implies that the meetings of the nomadic tribes for trading purposes were periodic affairs when he states that the Arapaho, Kaskaias, Kiowa, Comanche and Cheyenne "at distant periods, held a kind of fair on a tributary of the Platte, near the mountains (hence called Grand Camp Creek), at which they obtained British merchandize from the Shiennes of Shienne River (Cheyenne River of South Dakota), who obtained the same at the Mandan village from the British traders..."[30]

An additional indication of the fact that the Arapaho traded their horses to the Cheyenne is given by Fowler whose party was in a tremendous encampment of Southern Plains tribes on the Arkansas River where it is joined by the Apishapa. In November and December of 1821, there gathered here over seven hundred lodges of Kiowa, Comanche, Arapaho, Snake and Cheyenne, the combined total of whose horses, according to Fowler, amounted to twenty thousand. Yet in spite of this population, he states that "Between 400 and 500 horses have been stolen from them since we arrived and mostly from the pens in the center of the village surrounded by upwards of seven hundred lodges of watchful Indians..."[31] But there is no indication as to who stole them. What is of particular interest, however, is that the "... Arapaho have but a few in comparison with the others owing to their having last summer traded with Chians of the Missouri", and he goes on to state that "... the (Comanche) and Kiowa have great numbers of very fine horses – and equal to any I have ever known."[32]

Division of the Cheyenne

We see here what appears to be a distinction between the Cheyenne in this encampment and those of the Missouri. However, in the light of other information concerning the number of Cheyenne in the Southern Plains during this period, Fowler's statement that there were "about 200 lodges" of Cheyenne[33] in this encampment is puzzling. When, in

[29] Mackenzie in Masson, 1889, p. 346.
[30] James in Thwaites, 1906, Vol. XVII, p. 156.
[31] Fowler, 1898, p. 60. I have revised somewhat Fowler's original orthography.
[32] Ibid., p. 65.   [33] Ibid., p. 59.

1820, Long's expedition came upon a camp of Kiowa, Kaskaia, Arapaho, and Cheyenne, James wrote that the last named group "who have united their destiny with (the Arapaho) are a band of seceders from their own nation; and some time since, on the occurrence of a serious dispute with their kindred on Shienne river of the Missouri, flew their country, and placed themselves under the protection of the Bear Tooth (The Arapaho chief)."[34] However, there is no indication that the population was anywheres near as large as two hundred lodges. Nevertheless, the Rev. Morse, in his report to the Secretary of War for 1820, writes that "A small band of this tribe, (say 200) reside near the head of the Chien river. Sometime since they left their own nation and attached themselves to the Arrapahuys. They are bad fellows, faithless, and fond of plunder."[35] That these were the same Cheyenne who were met by Long in the same year seems to be indicated by their connection with the Arapaho. The band in question was undoubtedly dominated by a powerful leader, and it was probably because of his influence that they left their kinsmen in the north; for James states that when practically the entire population of the Kiowa, Arapaho, Cheyenne and Kaskaia bands crowded about Long's party, the latter

> ... requested the chiefs to direct their people to retire, with which request they immediately complied, but with the exception of the Shienne chief, were not obeyed. All the Shiennes forthwith left us, in compliance with the peremptory orders of their chief, who seems to be a man born to command, and to be endowed with a spirit of unconquerable ferocity, and capable of inflicting exemplary punishment upon any one who should dare to disobey his orders... The other chiefs seemed to possess only the dignity of office, without the power of command; the result, probably, of a deficiency of that native energy with which their companion was so pre-eminently endowed. They scarcely dared to reiterate their admonitions to their followers...[36]

A man with such will, determination, and qualities of leadership, was easily capable of coming into conflict with other tribal leaders and asserting his independence by withdrawing from the rest of the group with his followers. There seems to be no clue to, or mention of, this specific situation in any of the rest of the literature.[37]

[34] James in Thwaites, 1906, Vol. XVI, p. 211.

[35] Morse, 1822, p. 254.

[36] James in Thwaites, 1906, Vol. XVI, p. 198.

[37] Instances in which a number of Cheyenne have followed an influential leader into what may be termed temporary exile are not unknown in Cheyenne history. Grinnell cites the case of Buffalo Chief who, after having murdered another Cheyenne, was "... ordered to leave the camp. He gathered together all his relations and friends and they went off and for a long time camped by themselves, for now Buffalo Chief was an outlaw. At length, after they had been out away from the main camp for a long time, the people of Buffalo Chief's camp began to avoid the other people whom they met; they were shy about speaking to them. Hence they were called *Tatoimanah*, the shy or backward band"

If these references to some Cheyenne in the Southern Plains at this time are a harbinger of the division into northern and southern divisions of the tribe which occurred about ten or twelve years later, the evidence is not at all clear. According to the information given Grinnell by Porcupine Bull "... the Cheyennes, Arapahoes and part of the Atsena and some of the Blackfeet moved south of the Platte in 1826, or about that year, and began making raids on the Kiowas and Comanches, who lived south of the Arkansas."[38]

Now, we know from General Atkinson's report on the Treaty of 1825, with regard to the Cheyenne, that "Their principal rendezvous is towards the Black Hills, and their trading ground at the mouth of Cherry river, a branch of the Cheyenne, 40 miles above its mouth."[39] This would clearly place the Cheyenne north of the Platte, though there seem to be earlier indications that they did not confine themselves to this boundary at all times. Henry, writing in 1806, said that they generally spent the winter south of the Black Hills where "... they say, is the source of two large rivers; one runs to the N.E. and the other to the S.; the former falls into the Missouri, below the Pawnee village, I believe, under the name of Riviere Platte; the other, of course, into the Gulf of Mexico. Near the sources of these two rivers they make their annual hunts of bear and beaver, in company with the (Arapaho) ... a very numerous nation inhabiting that part of the country."[40] In 1802, Perrin Du Lac stated that they also hunted in the vicinity of the Platte. Henry would appear to be referring to the territory between the Platte and the Arkansas, although he may have been jumping to conclusions about the latter river. It is barely possible that the two rivers may have been only the north and south branches of the Platte.

With regard to the Arapaho, Henry seems to indicate that their regular habitat was south of the Platte. In 1820, James wrote that the Kaskaias, Arapaho, Kiowa, Bald-heads (Comanche), "a few Shoshones or Snakes," and the problematical band of Cheyennes "... are supposed to comprise nearly the whole erratic population of the country about the sources of the Platte and Arkansas; ..."[41] and that the Kiowa, Arapaho,

(1923b, Vol. I, p. 98). Llewellyn and Hoebel, in their analysis of this case, make the following statement: "The prestige and power of the man, however, is seen in the result of his magnetic influence in drawing a large number of innocent Cheyennes into exile with him. In this action may be seen also one way in which a new Cheyenne band was formed — a powerful and popular leader followed into involuntary (in this case) or voluntary separation from the tribe, plus an occasion, such as the prolonged exile — for — murder period, for continuing the new grouping until it had acquired a cohesion of its own, and its members had lost their older ties" (1941, p. 103).

[38] Grinnell, 1923a, p. 31.   [39] Atkinson, 1826, p. 10.
[40] Henry in Coues, 1897, pp. 383—384.
[41] James in Thwaites, 1906, Vol. XVI, p. 56.

Kaskaias, and the Cheyenne secessionists "... have been for the three years past (since 1817) wandering on the head waters and tributaries of Red river, having returned to the Arkansa only the day which preceded our first interview with them, on their way to the mountains at the sources of the Platte river. They ... constantly rove ... in pursuit of the herds of bisons in the vicinity of the sources of the Platte, Arkansa, and Red rivers."[42]

Thomas Fitzpatrick, the first Indian agent of the Upper Platte and Arkansas, wrote as follows in his report for 1847:

> The Chyennes ... claim (the Arkansas River) and on it about fifty miles above this place (i.e. Bent's Fort), have already selected a place for their settlement. But if the right of preemption stands good, the Aripahoes have much the best right, as they occupied this country long before the Chyennes ever saw it. Twenty years ago (1827) the Aripahoes were in possession of this country, and north to the South Fork of Platte and beyond, without any tribe to dispute their claim. The Chyennes at that time were living on the south side of Missouri river, between the Chyenne and White rivers, and along the Black Hills.[43]

This places the Cheyenne in the same vicinity as Atkinson did in 1825.

Thus all the evidence seems to place the Arapaho in the area between the Platte and the Arkansas well before the time Grinnell's informant claims that they moved south of the Platte in company with the Cheyenne. Furthermore, it is indicated by both James and Fowler that the Arapaho had friendly relations with the Kiowa and Comanche. Even the Cheyenne, as we have seen, brought parties of Kiowa and Comanche, or at least were present with them, among the Upper Missouri villages for trading purposes.

In 1826, or thereabouts, we are told by Porcupine Bull, the Cheyenne and Arapaho "began making raids on the Kiowas and Comanches, who lived south of the Arkansas."[44] It is at this time also that the Southern Cheyenne begin to be distinguished from their northern kinsmen. At any rate, Fitzpatrick states that it was pressure from the Sioux which forced the Cheyenne below the Platte around 1827 or later,[45] while Grinnell's information substantially agrees with this date.

Robinson says that the division of the Cheyenne occurred in about 1830 "... on account of a wish on the part of a portion of the tribe to follow the fur traders. One division migrated to the valleys of the Platte and Arkansas rivers and became known as the Southern Cheyenne. That portion that remained in their old possessions were designated the Northern Cheyenne ..."[46] The traders referred to were the Bent brothers and St. Vrain, and according to Grinnell, it was probably in 1828 (during the time when they were being pressed by the Sioux) that the Cheyenne met them on the Arkansas River in southeastern Colorado.

[42] *Ibid.*, p. 211. [43] Hafen, 1932, p. 134. [44] Grinnell, 1923a, p. 31.
[45] Hafen, 1932, p. 134. [46] Robinson, 1902, editorial note 85, p. 147.

The Bents were encamped at the mouth of the Purgatoire, or had a stockade there, and to this place came a party of Cheyenne who had been south (i. e. below the Arkansas) catching wild horses and were returning north to their camp. Porcupine Bull stated that the leaders of this party were Yellow Wolf, Little Wolf and Wolf Chief, and that it was at this meeting that Yellow Wolf made friends with the Bents and gave them names. The question of trade was also discussed, and Yellow Wolf told the Bents that a post on the Arkansas near the mountains was too far from the buffalo range for the Indians to frequent. He suggested that the Bents and St. Vrain build a post near the mouth of the Purgatoire, and said that if they would do this he would bring his band and others there to trade. It is said that Charles Bent at once accepted the chief's proposal and that this was how Bent's Fort came to be built.

The Bent brothers and Ceran St. Vrain began this large fort in 1828, but it was not completed until 1832...[47]

Further distinguishing not only between the Northern and Southern Cheyenne, but also between similar divisions of the Arapaho, Grinnell states that Fort St. Vrain, built by the same traders on the South Platte, a short distance below St. Vrain's Fork, was "intended for the trade of the northern Indians; that is, for the Sioux and the northern bands of Cheyennes and Arapahoes, who seldom got down south as far as the Arkansas river and so did not often come to Bent's Fort, and indeed did much of their trading at Fort Laramie, on the Platte."[48]

Viewing the facts as stated here, they would seem to indicate that the division of the Cheyenne into northern and southern groups took place for reasons of trade in approximately 1830 or shortly thereafter.[49] It may also be that the marriage of William Bent in about 1835 to Owl Woman, who was the daughter of White Thunder, keeper of the medicine arrows, had something further to do with accentuating the division of the tribe. Although the great westward trails and the building of the Union Pacific Railroad were yet to make final the division of the buffalo into northern and southern herds, it may be that this separation of the herds was already beginning to make itself subtly felt as early as the 1830's. However, the picture in this regard is not at all clear, and it is undoubtedly true that a complex of factors were involved in the formation of northern and southern divisions of the Cheyenne. There does not seem to be any evidence of how, and on what basis, the separation actually took place, and the only specific reason given for it in the literature is that of a desire on a part of the tribe to take advantage of the practically exclusive trade facilities offered by the building of Bent's Fort on the Arkansas River along the Santa Fe Trail.

[47] Grinnell, 1923a, p. 31.   [48] *Ibid.*, pp. 41—42.
[49] Scott, relying exclusively on the evidence provided by James' Account of Long's Expedition, as cited in the present study, maintains that "... the Northern and Southern Cheyenne separated at least as early as 1816, and probably earlier;..." (1907, p. 60).

From this period on, the available historical data, as far as the present problem is concerned, refer only to the Southern Cheyenne. The northern division of the tribe becomes one of the many Indian groups who traded at the various posts established on the Upper Missouri and its tributaries. At the same time, the earlier trade relations between the Cheyenne and Arikara have become dissipated, partly because of the increasing White trade on the Missouri, and partly as a result of the southward movement of the Cheyenne. Additional factors of consequence may be the continued hostility of the Sioux against the Arikara and the devastating results of the Leavenworth campaign against the same tribe.[50]

Bent's Fort and the Southern Plains Tribes

Whether it was the increasing pressure of tribes from the north; whether it was the increasing competition among the tribes of the Northern Plains for the commerce of the trading posts which were springing up along the Missouri and the Yellowstone; whether the Cheyenne saw the opportunity to withdraw from the latter situation by taking advantage of the relatively exclusive facilities offered by Bent's Fort, they seem to have made common cause with the Arapaho in the territory between the Platte and the Arkansas by about 1830. From this time on, the Kiowa, Comanche and Apache had as their northern boundary the Arkansas River, which they crossed only at the risk of hostilities with the Cheyenne. Perhaps the Arapaho were forced by circumstances rather than preference into a closer alliance with the Cheyenne, for they, too, reaped the benefits of the trade at Bent's Fort.

According to Grinnell:

At the time of the building of Bent's Fort (1832), the upper Arkansas river was not only the boundary between the United States and Mexico, but was also the dividing line between two hostile groups of plains tribes. To the south of the river lived the Kiowas, Comanches and Prairie Apaches; to the north were the Southern Cheyennes and Arapahoes; and for many years these two groups were actively at war with each other.

During the early thirties none of these tribes appear to have considered the valley of the Arkansas its home. The river and its valley was a danger zone constantly being crossed by war parties. At that period the Southern Cheyennes were newcomers in the southern country which lay between the South Platte and the Arkansas, and they did not often move their camps down to the Arkansas until after the completion of Bent's Fort... The Southern Arapahoes ranged more or less with the Cheyennes, but seem to have kept nearer the mountains...[51]

The Cheyenne, as we saw, claim credit for the final location of the trading post, and although the Bents certainly had a vital interest in the Indian trade, there were also other practical factors they had to consider.

[50] DeLand, 1906, pp. 480ff.   [51] Grinnell, 1923a, pp. 68—69.

Chittenden says, "It was the great crossroads station of the southwest. The north and the south route between the Platte river country and Santa Fe, and the east and west route up the Arkansas and into the mountains found it their most natural trading point."[52] And again he writes, "The Bent brothers first built a stockade near the mouth of Fountain Creek, but afterward moved downstream (at the behest of the Cheyenne ?) where they would be more in line with the trade between the United States and Taos on the mountain branch of the Santa Fe Trail. The fort was thus in touch with the trade of Santa Fe and that of the mountains."[53] Although Chittenden claims it was founded in 1829, Farnham writing in 1839, states that it was erected in 1832 "... for purposes of trade with the Spaniards of Santa Fe and Taos, and the Eutaw, Cheyenne and Cumanche Indians."[54] As regards the trade of the latter tribe with the Bents, we are told by Grinnell that "Adobe Fort was built on the South Canadian, at the request of the chiefs of the Kiowas, Comanches and Apaches. Before peace was made between these tribes and the Cheyennes and Arapahoes, in 1840, the three tribes that lived south of the Arkansas were usually afraid to visit Bent's Fort to trade, lest they should there meet a large camp of their enemies."[55] From this statement it seems to be clear that the Kiowa, Comanche and Apache were pretty effectively contained below the Arkansas River. Grinnell goes on to say, however, that:

> William Bent and the traders were naturally especially anxious that there should be no collisions near the fort. Each tribe would expect the trader to take its part, and this could not be done without incurring the enmity of the other tribes. The trader wished to be on good terms with all, and this William Bent accomplished with singular discretion. Although he had a Cheyenne wife, he was on excellent terms, and always remained so, with the enemies of the Cheyennes.[56]

Perhaps because they were related to Bent by marriage, the Cheyenne seemed to have had a good deal of liberty at the post and were apparently permitted to roam through it at will. They were certainly more at home there than any other tribe, as is plain from Lt. Abert's report[57] and Garrard's account.[58] Thus, although, as Grinnell says, "... Bent's Fort lay in the danger zone between the two groups and was constantly visited by war parties of both sides"[59] and although the Bents succeeded in maintaining the friendship of both sides, in actual practice it was the Cheyenne who were in possession, so to speak, whereas the Kiowa or Comanche might pay fleeting visits to the fort in small parties when the Cheyenne were not around. Large scale Indian trading at the fort took place chiefly with the Cheyenne and Arapaho.

[52] Chittenden, 1935, Vol. 2, p. 539.   [53] *Ibid.*, p. 943.
[54] Farnham in Thwaites, 1906, Vol. XXVIII, p. 161.
[55] Grinnell, 1923a, p. 42.   [56] *Ibid.*   [57] Abert, 1848.
[58] Garrard, 1938.   [59] Grinnell, 1923a, p. 69.

The two items of native production that were of any importance in the trade at Bent's Fort were buffalo robes and horses (including mules). As a matter of fact, these commodities may be said to have been practically the entire basis of the trade, and they had their season. When the trade in buffalo robes terminated in the spring, it was replaced by that in horses and mules. All these items were shipped to St. Louis by the Bents, and although they relied almost entirely on the Indians for the furs, their trade with them in animals was supplemented by the journeys of the White traders to New and Old Mexico where they purchased large herds.

It might be of interest, at this point, to quote extensively from Grinnell's account of the manner of trade and articles involved in the commercial transactions between Bent's traders and the Indians.

> Each of these traders (employed by Bent) had especially friendly relations with some particular tribe of Indians, and each was naturally sent to the tribe that he knew best. Besides this, often when villages of Indians came and camped somewhere near the post, the chiefs would ask that a particular man be sent to their village to trade with them. Sometimes to a very large village two or three traders might be sent, the work being more than one man could handle in a short period of time. Maxwell seems to have traded most frequently with the Arapahoes, while John Smith was usually sent to the Cheyenne camps, as he is said to have understood and spoken the Cheyenne language better than any of the other traders...
>
> ... the trade in robes ended in the spring, and during the summer the traders often went to the different Indian villages to barter for horses and mules.
>
> When the trader reached an Indian camp he went to the lodge of a chief or principal man, with whom he stayed and under whose protection he placed his goods. Soon after his arrival the crier went about the camp calling out the news of the trader's arrival, announcing what goods he had brought and what he wished to trade for. Thus when Garrard visited the Cheyenne camp with Smith, the crier called out that Smith had come to trade for mules, and had brought tobacco, blue blankets, black (deep blue) blankets, white blankets, coffee, etc...
>
> ... a great trade went on also in horses and mules of which the Indians possessed great numbers and of which they were always getting more. The Indians constantly paid for their goods with these animals...[60]

On some occasions, when the wild horses which had been purchased from the Indians had been broken by the Mexicans employed at the fort, they might be taken to Taos and Santa Fe to be sold there or be resold to the Indians in exchange for buffalo robes.

One of the most important bases of the antagonism between the Cheyenne and Arapaho on one side and the Kiowa and Comanche on the other, was apparently the necessity for the former tribes to supply the rapidly expanding market for horses, which were required at St. Louis and Independence to outfit expeditions and migrants to the west. As was pointed out earlier the source of supply of horses was in the Spanish

[60] *Ibid.*, pp. 58, 60.

5*

Southwest and Mexico to which the Comanche, together with the Kiowa
and Apache formed a barrier. The Cheyenne and Arapaho had either to
break through the barrier, a most difficult and dangerous feat, or steal
the horses from the tribes south of the Arkansas. And so the Kiowa,
Kiowa-Apache, Comanche, and Prairie-Apache "usually kept well south
of the Arkansas in order to avoid, as far as possible, the raiding parties of
Cheyennes and Arapahoes, who were constantly trying to take horses
from them . . ."[61]

Just how powerful a factor the desire for horses had become for some
Cheyenne during this period is shown by an incident which occurred in
1837, as related by Grinnell. The Bow String Soldiers desired to form a
war party to head south and seek out a Kiowa or Comanche camp for the
purpose of stealing horses and perhaps take some scalps. However, a
Cheyenne had previously killed another member of the tribe, and until
the medicine arrows had been renewed in the proper ceremonial fashion
they could not depart and expect their efforts to be attended by success.
The Bow String men, in an impatient mood, ". . . wished the arrows to
be renewed so that they might set out at once, but when they spoke to
Gray (Painted) Thunder, the arrow keeper, about it he told them that
the time and place were not propitious and advised them not to go.
There was much dispute about this, but at length the Bow String
soldiers told Gray Thunder that he must renew the arrows. He refused;
whereupon, the soldiers attacked and beat him with their quirts and
quirt-handles until he promised to renew the arrows for them. Gray
Thunder was then an old man, over seventy. He renewed the arrows as
ordered, but before the ceremony he warned the Bow String men that
the first time they went to war they would have bad fortune." Although
a Southern Arapaho sun-dance pledger prophesied a big war party *after*
the dance, another man had visions of blood at this time and warned
everybody not to go. "Most of the people listened to what this man said,
but, nevertheless, small parties of young men began to steal away from
camp, for the Cheyennes . . . were likely to undertake it even though
they disregarded the ceremonies and violated the oldest laws." Every
last man of the expedition, which set out on foot, was killed.[62]

Although it should not be inferred that trade was by itself directly
responsible for the weakening of religious and ceremonial beliefs as
exemplified in the foregoing situation, it must be regarded as an important factor in a complex of influences producing subtle changes. Though
wealth, reckoned largely in terms of horses, brought with it influence
and prestige which were desirable and approved goals, it was still the
means for securing the material goods desired by the Indians. Inasmuch
as the quest for horses cannot be separated from the trade situation
which was enmeshed in the warp and weft of Indian life, it must bear its

    [61] *Ibid.*, p. 69.   [62] Grinnell, 1915, p. 69.

share of the responsibility, though it is not mensurable. There were numerous occasions among the Cheyenne when horses were given away, and these manifestations of generosity conferred honor and prestige on the donor; but it would be difficult to relate the acquisition of horses directly to these occasions alone as a motivating factor. The significance of trade loomed too large in the economy for simpliste explanations.

A number of men went to war without any motivation for taking scalps, but only for the purpose of taking horses. Though they lacked the war honors that came with the taking of scalps and the counting of coup, they nevertheless were highly regarded for their ability to capture and accumulate wealth in horses. In this connection, Grinnell writes that:

> ... there were many brave and successful warriors of the Cheyenne who ... on their war journeys tried to avoid coming in close contact with enemies, and had no wish to kill enemies. Such men went to war for the sole purpose of increasing their possessions by capturing horses; that is, they carried on war as a business — for profit. Some of these — men who possessed high reputation for courage, success, and general well-doing — made it their boast that they had never killed a man, and perhaps had never counted a coup. Such men specialized in capturing horses: their interest in was lay in that alone...
>
> Men famous for success in this particular field of war were Old Yellow Wolf, who lived in the first half of the nineteenth century, and was killed at Sand Creek; Big Foot, who died about 1901, and Elk River, who died about 1908. All these men lived to great age; all were successful in war, and all had great reputations as being most skillful in dealing with enemies and securing horses...
>
> Elk River had a remarkable life. He was never a doctor; never was in a sweat house; never took part in ceremonies. He just lived his life, took care of his family, and held the respect of the whole tribe. He was a most generous man, and at the same time a man with a remarkable sense of justice. He was a skillful catcher of wild horses...[63]

The case of Yellow Wolf may also be cited as an example of a chief who was practical in his attitude toward the acquisition of horses. He did not wish to be deterred from his objective by failure to perform properly the ceremonies required of the leader of a war party along the route, and consequently he dispensed with them entirely.

> 'These ceremonies,' he said, 'oblige us to avoid too many things. If we should fail to observe some law or some custom we might be obliged to turn back. On this trip I will get my own water and cook my own food, and in these matters will be just like any of you. But I wish you to remember that I am still the head of this party.'
>
> Yellow Wolf was a great general, a great planner. He seldom, or never, went to war for scalps, but was a noted taker of horses. He was very successful in catching wild horses and in capturing horses from the Kiowas and Comanches. He seemed to know always where the Comanches would be at certain times of the year, and would set out to get horses from them. Elk River, also very successful in such enterprises, discarded these ceremonies in the same way.[64]

[63] Grinnell, 1923b, Vol. 2, pp. 2—3.   [64] *Ibid.*, pp. 13—14.

The Kiowa-Comanche Situation

The intensity of hostilities between the Cheyenne-Arapaho and the Kiowa-Comanche allies mounted steadily in the decade 1830—1840, and reached the peak in 1838 at the battle of Wolf Creek, where the latter tribes w ʾre defeated. In addition to these enemies north of the Arkansas, the Kioʾ ʾa and Comanche were embroiled in hostilities in their own territory, soʾ ʾth of that line, as a result of increasing pressures which had begun to make themselves felt by about 1820 after the establishment of the Arkansas Territory.[65] Up until that time, in their relations with the Spaniards, the Comanche had control of the situation.

> The expanding Spanish empire stopped short when it reached the Great Plains. The San Saba mission project, which was the only effort of consequence made to encroach on the Comanchería, failed and had to be abandoned. The Spaniards were not even able to protect their settlements founded within reach of the Comanches, much less to subdue the Indians themselves. Comparative peace prevailed in New Mexico because the Indians found it profitable to trade with these settlements while they preyed on those farther south. The end of a century of conflict found the Indians victors in every respect. Their country had been enlarged, and the Indians they had displaced had been hurled back on the settlements to add to the problems of the white people. The savages not only held the South Plains but made life and property unsafe in communities hundreds of miles south and west of the Rio Grande.
>
> The Comanches rather than the Spaniards had come to be the aggressors. Their raids extended farther and farther into the north Mexican settlements, and were more destructive than when they were first begun... To cope successfully with these fierce warriors of the plains called for more money, more men, and greater resourcefulness than that associated with the Spanish effort during the last three or four decades of the empire. The efforts of the new Mexican government were not one whit more effective.[66]

Thus, although the Comanches received from time to time Spanish presents, which were given in an effort to help the peace, and although they engaged in sporadic trade with other tribes and occasional traders, Comanche territory had been free from foreign incursions and domination. They made war at will, and depended on this means to secure such European goods and supplies as they desired, rather than upon trade. When, after the beginning of the nineteenth century some Anglo-Americans began coming into their territory to trade arms, ammunition and other goods for horses, they dealt with them, but there were no posts established in their territory.

When Fowler and Long were in Comanche country in 1820 and 1821, of all the tribes they met, the Comanche were most hostile in their attitude. By 1825, the removal of eastern Indians to the eastern borders of Comanche territory was beginning to gain momentum; and by the

[65] Foreman, 1926, p. 57.   [66] Richardson, 1933, p. 75.

end of the decade White settlers were moving farther westward from the Arkansas territory.[67]

> About 1832 war and confusion seemed to be increasing in the country west of Indian territory between the Arkansas and Red rivers. The plains tribes were fighting the one with the other, intruding Indians from the east were going into the prairies and antagonizing the native Indians by killing their game, and the Great Plains country was anything but safe for the few white persons who dared to enter it.[68]

Although the government of 1832 and 1833 sent unsuccessful expeditions into the Comanche country, Leavenworth and Dodge finally established successful contact with the Indians and paved the way for a treaty at Camp Holmes in 1835. This, however, was soon abrogated by the Indians when they learned it permitted the border Indians to hunt and kill game in their territory.[69]

In 1836, the northern bands of the Comanche joined with the Kiowa "in one of the most destructive raids ever made along the Texas frontier," and during the warfare between Texas and Mexico in 1836 and 1837, the latter side was inciting the Indians against the Whites. The Mexicans claimed the Texans were bent upon taking the Indian lands, and the Indians soon came to see the truth of it themselves. When President Burnet of Texas sent Major Le Grand to negotiate a treaty with the northern bands of Comanches, Chief Traveling Wolf told that officer that "... so long as he continued to see the gradual approach of the whites and their habitations to the hunting grounds of the Comanches, so long would he believe to be true what the Mexicans had told him, viz., that the ultimate intention of the white man was to deprive them of their country; and so long would he continue to be the enemy of the white race."[70]

By 1838, "the land offices of the (Texas) republic had been opened, people from the United States were coming by the thousands, and the Comanche country ... was disturbed all along its eastern and southern fringe by daring men who carried instruments that 'stole the land.' "[71]

In May of 1838, General Johnston tried to negotiate a treaty with the Comanches. "While he tried to discuss the great advantages of peace with the whites and the benefits to be derived from trade between the two races, the Indians persisted in claiming some interest in the land they had occupied for nearly a century, and told him plainly that *they did not want trading posts in their country.*"[72]

---

[67] Foreman, 1926, p. 57 ff.
[68] Richardson, 1933, p. 79.
[69] *Ibid.*, pp. 80—86.
[70] *Ibid.*, p. 93. Extract from Le Grand's report of April 26, 1837, cited in Yoakum, History of Texas, Vol. II, pp. 228 ff.
[71] *Ibid.*, p. 96.   [72] *Ibid.*, (italics mine).

Mirabeau B. Lamar, who became President of the republic in December of 1838, favored a war policy against the Indians. In that same month and in January 1839, the Texas Congress passed acts which "provided for a system of frontier forts, authorized the placing of over a thousand men in the field and appropriated a million dollars to be used in the defense of the country."[73] So now the Kiowa and Comanche became involved in a series of wars with the Texans, at least until 1840 when those tribes made peace with the Cheyenne and Arapaho.

In addition to their troubles with the Whites and the encroachment of the eastern Indians on to their hunting lands, game began to become scarce.

> As early as 1833 explorers and adventurers had begun to observe that the range of the buffalo along the Arkansas and Canadian rivers and the country between was rapidly growing narrower. In 1833 Latrobe's party had to go one hundred miles beyond the Arkansas boundary to find any buffalo... At the same time, another writer made substantially the same statement, and commented on the rapidity with which the animal receded before the approach of civilization. He stated: 'Ten years since they abounded in the vicinity of Fort Gibson; ... they have receded, it would seem one hundred miles westward in the last ten years;...'[74]

Although the buffalo were far from depleted in the range of the Comanche, the factor of a diminishing supply of the animal so essential to the life of the people, is mentioned here as a possible subtle ecological change in the complex of circumstances by which the Comanche and Kiowa were being affected during this period.

Thus, by 1840, we see the Kiowa, Comanche, and Prairie Apache, their allies, engaged in hostilities on the periphery of their territory to the north, east and south. They were reaching a critical period where a decision had to be made. The advance of the well-armed eastern Indians and the Whites was an overwhelming tide, and to compromise for peace in this quarter would only mean accepting the terms of the Whites and surrendering their lands. The best alternative, then, seemed to be to make peace on their northern borders with the Cheyenne and Arapaho where they could acquire the advantage of trade which would supply them with the arms necessary to carry on their struggle against the forces invading their territory.

The Great Peace

Whereas the Cheyenne account of the great peace made with the Kiowa, Comanche and Prairie Apache is replete with detail, all we find from the Kiowa side is little more than a passing reference to the occasion. Mooney states that "According to the Kiowa account, the first overtures were made by the Cheyenne, who sent two delegates with

---

[73] *Ibid.*, p. 104.   [74] *Ibid.*, pp. 173—174.

proposals, but the Kiowas were suspicious and sent them back. The Cheyenne then made a second attempt, with more success, and a peace was concluded."[75] However, the weight of the evidence with regard to the historical situation of both sides to the peace, when taken together with the precise account recorded by Grinnell, seems to lend more credence to the Cheyenne version of the peace.[76]

According to the Cheyenne, then, ". . . some Apaches came to the Arapaho camp and told them that the Kiowas and Comanches were camped on the Beaver River – the north fork of the North Canadian – and wished to make peace with the Cheyennes and Arapahoes. The visiting Apaches were staying in the lodge of Bull, a noted Arapaho chief.

"At this time a war party of eight Cheyennes, under the leadership of Seven Bulls, was in the Arapaho camp, having stopped there on their way south to take horses from the Kiowas, Comanches and Apaches."

The peace proposals were presented to the Cheyenne war party by the Arapaho chief, and they returned immediately to carry the message back to their chiefs. Bull told them that ". . . if you will make peace they will bring back to you the heads (scalps) of those Bow String soldiers, wrapped up in a cloth. They will also give you many horses – horses to the men, and also to the women and children." The Cheyenne were thus given the practical inducement of obtaining horses.

After the war party delivered the message to the Cheyenne camp on Shawnee creek, a tributary of the Republican, ". . . the chiefs discussed the matter, and it was finally agreed that a decision should be left to the Dog Soldiers, as they were the strongest and bravest of the soldier bands." The two bravest Dog Soldiers were sent for, presented with the peace proposals and were told to talk it over with the Dog Soldiers ". . . and let us know what you think of it; what is best to be done." The two delegates convened the Dog Soldiers, reported to them and concluded that it was their ". . . opinion that our chiefs are in favor of making peace with the Kiowas, Comanches and Apaches . . . what do you all think about it ?" The soldiers agreed that it should be left up to the two leaders, who thereupon decided in favor of peace and brought their decision back to the council of chiefs. The chiefs all stood up and thanked the Dog Soldiers, for "They were glad to have the peace made."

The people were informed and forbidden to go on war parties against the other three tribes who were notified to meet the Cheyenne and Arapaho about fifty miles below Bent's Fort, at the mouth of Two Butte Creek on the south side of the Arkansas. "Then the whole camp moved toward the (Bent's) Fort, for they were anxious to trade for many things in order to make presents to the Kiowas, Comanches, and Apaches."

[75] Mooney, 1898, p. 276.
[76] Grinnell, 1915, Chapter VI. All subsequent quotations concerning this event are taken from Grinnell's account.

Later, at the appointed place, four Kiowas and a boy, two Comanches, and an Apache came to the Cheyenne camp, smoked the pipe ceremonially, and "Thus the peace was declared."

Though the Kiowas brought the scalps of the forty-two Bow String Soldier :, they were told by High-Backed Wolf, the Cheyenne chief: "Frien :, these things if shown and talked about will only make bad feeling. The peace is made now; take the heads away with you and use them as you think best; do not let us see them or hear of them."

When High-Backed Wolf told the people that peace was now made, he added: ". . . if any of you have any presents that you wish to give these men, bring them here." And Little Mountain, the principal Kiowa said: "We all of us have many horses; as many as we need; we do not wish to accept any horses as presents, but we will be glad to receive any other gifts. We, the Kiowas, Comanches, and Apaches, have made a road to give many horses to you when we all come here." The Cheyenne then came forward with their presents and surrounded the Kiowa boy with blankets up to his head.

The chiefs then agreed to meet on the Arkansas just below Bent's Fort, the Cheyenne and Arapaho to camp on the north side of the river, and the others on the south side. When the tribes had met and feasted in the Cheyenne camp, the Kiowa invited all to cross the river to their camp the next day and to come on foot, for they would all return on horseback.

The next day they all waded across the river, women and all, and sat in rows, the men in front and the women and children behind them. The first Kiowa to come up was Sa tank'. He had a bundle of sticks too big to hold in the hand, so he carried them in the hollow of his left arm. He began at one end of the row of men and went along, giving a stick to each. At length when all the sticks had been given away he went to some brush and broke off a good many more. Mountain said: 'Do not lose those sticks. We do not know your names, but as soon as we get through you must come up and get your horses.' All the other Kiowas gave many horses, but Sa tank' gave the most; they say that he gave away two hundred and fifty horses.

Some unimportant men and women received four, five, or six horses, but the chiefs received the most. The Cheyennes did not have enough ropes to lead back their horses; they were obliged to drive them across in bunches. The Kiowas, Comanches and Apaches had sent their Mexican captives and their young men to bring in their horses from the hills and hold them close to the lodges, and they would walk along with the Cheyennes and point to one after another saying: 'I give you that one; I give *you* that one.' . . .

The next day the people of the three tribes crossed the river, and entered the circle of the Cheyenne camp, where they sat down in rows. The chiefs of the three tribes sat in front. Then the Cheyenne women brought out the food in kettles and everybody ate. At that time, of civilized foods the Cheyennes had only rice, dried apples, and cornmeal, and to sweeten their food they had New Orleans molasses. They had no coffee and no sugar. But this food that the Cheyennes had was strange to the people from the south, and they liked it.

After all had eaten, High-Backed Wolf called out to his people that now their guests were through eating and they should bring their presents. 'Those of you who are bringing guns must fire them in front of the lodges; not here close to these people.' He spoke to the chief guests, saying: 'Do not be frightened if you hear shots; it is our custom when we are going to give a gun to anyone to fire it in the air.' Then for a little while it sounded like a battle in the Cheyenne camp — a great firing of guns. The Cheyennes brought guns, blankets, calico, beads, brass kettles — many presents.

After all these had been presented, High-Backed Wolf said to the guests: 'Now, we have made peace, and we have finished making presents to one another; tomorrow we will begin to trade with each other. Your people can come here and try to trade for the things that you like, and my people will go to your camp to trade.' It was so done, and this was the beginning of a great trade.

The peace then made has never been broken.

In view of the historical situation at the time, it is entirely logical that the initiative for peace should have come from the southern tribes. In fact, the affairs of all the Indians in their relations with the Whites were approaching a crisis which burst forth in the period of the Indian wars and culminated in the last desperate hope of the Ghost Dance movement. The Cheyenne and Arapaho also saw the portent of the future and so they, too, were glad of the opportunity for a peace. Both sides reaped very definite advantages from the peace, the northern tribes being given access to a vast source of horses and the southerners to a regular supply of trade goods, not the least important of which were guns and ammunition. Though they raided and traded for these articles they never had a sufficient supply or a constant source for replacements and repairs. When in 1834, Catlin and Wheelock were among the Kiowa and Comanche they remarked how few guns these tribes had.[77] They were now entering a period when firearms were necessary to wage efficient war, and a free approach to Bent's Fort made them more accessible. This was, indeed, "the beginning of a great trade."

There are a number of factors of interest in this account. From the very beginning, the Apache emissaries clearly stated that many horses would be given to everyone – men, women and children, a most unusual stipulation.[78] And at various stages in the peace negotiations, this point was reiterated by the Kiowa. Mountain, the Kiowa Chief, emphasized that his allies did not wish any horses, but would be glad to accept any other gifts. This was tantamount to stating what the predominant articles of exchange would be – what the southern tribes wished from the Cheyenne and Arapaho. For we have already seen that the conventional

[77] Richardson, 1933, p. 87.

[78] See Henry's description, previously quoted, of the abortive peace ceremonies between the Cheyenne and Hidatsa, where the old Hidatsa officer stated ". . . that the Big Bellies were ready to give good guns and ammunition, but expected to receive good horses in return" (in Coues, 1897, p. 390).

trade with regard to guns or horses was implicit, in that when one of those two commodities was offered, the other was to be given in exchange.

Secondly, although the tribes speak of giving each other presents to cement the peace, it is, in fact, ceremonial trade on a tribal scale to initiate the period of individual trade to follow. High-Backed Wolf said at the conclusion of the peace-making exchange "... we have finished making presents to one another; to-morrow we will begin to trade with each other..." As in the instance of the Cheyenne and Hidatsa in 1806, the ceremonial trade appears to be a statement of the basic commodities the two groups may expect from each other in future transactions. But at the same time each party receives the goods for which it has immediate and urgent need.

Another point of interest is the clue provided to the enormous herds owned by some of the southern allies. The Kiowa chief, Sa tank', himself gave away two hundred and fifty horses. And on the Cheyenne side it was the chiefs who received most of these animals, unimportant people receiving as few as four.

Llewellyn and Hoebel, in their excellent study of Cheyenne law, have analyzed the legal aspects of the manner in which the decision for peace was arrived at between the council of chiefs and the Dog Soldiers.

> The proposition was no simple one. The Cheyenne had become dependent upon the horse, and any warrior's path to glory and wealth lay most easily and quickly in raids upon the rich horse herders of the south, these same Kiowas and Comanches. Acceptance of the proposal meant that the young men would be blocked in one of their main and favorite avenues of activity. Hostility with the Kiowas and Comanches had been unceasing for at least half a century. The alternative values to the Cheyennes are not clear to us, unless they lay in some scheme for trading horses, on which we lack information. The soldier interest in the case is obvious; no less obvious is the fact that it had the favorable aspect of coinciding with the interests of the whole Cheyenne tribe.[79]

It is true that the Cheyenne could now no longer raid the Kiowa and Comanche for horses. What they *could* do was raid the Spanish settlements in the southwest and Mexico, and this is precisely what they did. Fitzpatrick, in his report for 1847, wrote: "... Not long since I happened to meet with a party of Cheyennes, thirty-five in number, all young men,

[79] Llewellyn and Hoebel, 1941, p. 93. Actually, hostilities between these tribes and the Cheyenne had been only intermittent until the Cheyenne came down to the Arkansas about 1828. As a matter of fact, we saw That on many occassions as late as 1821, the two parties entered into peaceful trade relations. But as Grinnell (1915, p. 34) says, "Between 1826 and 1840 abitter warfare was waged between these parties of allies. This very likely arose from the need for horses, which they obtained chiefly from the south, and it is likely that the horse was an important cause for the southward movement of all these tribes."

and well mounted. I enquired of the chief where they were bound for, and what was their object, he very candidly told me they were bound for the frontier settlements of New Mexico for the purpose of plundering the scattering inhabitants. . . "[80] This was part of the "alternative values."

Thus, the "warrior's path to glory and wealth" was not blocked by the Peace, and at the same time the interests of the people were served. For, although the cultural ideals of masculine achievement had to have a means of expression, there were patterns and interests centered on intertribal trade which also required expression for the rest of the populace. Fortunately, both interests could be served, and perhaps this fact rendered the final decision easier to make.

[80] Hafen, 1932, p. 128.

CHAPTER FOUR

CONCLUSIONS: EFFECTS ON THE CHEYENNE

This study may be regarded, in a sense, as an examination of how international relations among the tribes of the Great Plains were influenced and affected by trade. The Cheyenne Indians have served mainly as a focus of interest to indicate the manner in which an individual tribe reacted, in terms of the trade situation, to the changing forces of history.

Summary. Coming out of an area of intense trade activity, both White and intertribal, in the northeastern forests, where they were an unimportant marginal tribe, the Cheyenne entered a new environment in the Great Plains, where they assumed an increasingly important role. Having penetrated the Plains in the vicinity of the Upper Missouri horticultural villages, they adopted, during a period of transition, a type of economy in which the horse was an all important instrument of production. At approximately the same time, they became involved in the developing trade situation in that region, especially after crossing the Missouri. Thus, the quest for horses to sustain a tribal economy based on buffalo hunting, became inextricably interwoven with the requirements of trade. The horse, consequently, became important from two points of view. First, it was an instrument of production to fulfill the basic subsistence requirements of food, shelter and clothing; and in this connection, too, it was of almost equal value as a beast of burden and a means of transportation. Secondly, from the viewpoint of trade, it was not only essential for the production of a surplus of skins, leather goods, meat, etc., beyond the needs of the group, but also, as a medium of exchange, it was the basic commodity traded for European goods.

It was, therefore, essential to produce a surplus of horses which was acquired both by trading and raiding. Raiding was the preferred method both among nomadic and horticultural tribes, for if the animals were acquired through trade, it meant having to give up much desired European goods in exchange. Since the nomadic tribes were in a better position to secure horses by raiding, they got most of their supply in this way, whereas the horticultural tribes of the Upper Missouri obtained the greater share of their animals by trade with the nomads.

Once the Cheyenne were established west of the Missouri, they were situated between separate sources of supply of exchangeable commodities. The supply of horses was fed northward into the Plains from Mexico and the Southwest, while European goods were flowing into the

area from Canada via the villages of the Upper Missouri. In this situation, the Cheyenne bridged the gap as a transmission belt by virtue of
their historical connections with the village groups through whose
territory they entered the Plains. At first, they performed this function
by introducing other nomadic tribes to the Upper Missouri village trade,
and, in the course of a few years, they brought the European goods
obtained from the village Indians to trade centers located in the Interior Plains where they met other nomadic tribes from whom they
obtained horses in exchange for European commodities.

However, the competition among the Missouri tribes for the trade of
the Whites became increasingly severe, with the result that warfare
among them was aggravated. All tried to retain a monopoly on the
supply of a trader's goods, and often forcibly attempted to interfere
with White commercial ventures along the reaches of the Missouri. The
situation there was further complicated by the turbulent operations of
the western bands of the Dakota, who, having a source of supply of guns
and other European goods in the Eastern Dakota on the Upper Mississippi, engaged in wholesale plunder of Indians and Whites on the
Missouri. Here they made virtual serfs of the Arikara who were the main
object of their depredations. Though the Arikara suffered oppression in
this relationship, they nevertheless depended upon the Sioux for their
supply of guns and other articles of British manufacture obtained
almost entirely on the terms set by their oppressors. Inasmuch as the
Arikara had to engage in a certain amount of trade in order to obtain
horses and other commodities which the Sioux demanded, they were
caught in a contradiction they could not resolve, for the Sioux attempted
to prevent other tribes from trading with the Arikara. Since the Cheyenne were one of the chief customers of the Arikara they often came into
conflict with the Sioux, who did not wish to see the Cheyenne supplied
with the arms and ammunition they had given to the Arikara. The
Sioux and the Cheyenne, historical enemies from the time the latter left
Minnesota, were again engaged over the concrete issue of competition
for advantages to be derived from the Arikara.

Trading for horses in the Interior Plains could not continue to be a
profitable venture to the Cheyenne, who obtained European goods not
directly from the White traders, but through the medium of the middleman village tribes. They therefore had to rely more heavily upon raiding
and so penetrated more and more into the Southern Plains as a result
both of necessity, to obtain a cheaper supply of horses, and under
pressure from the expanding Sioux. As a consequence of their penetra-
tion of the area between the Platte and Arkansas Rivers, they came into
open and bloody conflict with the Kiowa and Comanche, whose large
herds of horses were the object of increasing raids by the Cheyenne. At
about the same time, the establishment of Bent's Fort enabled the

Cheyenne more easily to give up their middleman role and trade directly with the Whites.

This situation apparently presented the Cheyenne with the choice of moving south permanently in a virtual monopoly of a source of European goods in combination with the Arapaho, or of continuing to pursue their fortunes in the Northern Plains, where they could trade together with many other tribes at the increasing number of trading posts which were being established in that region. Whatever was the true nature of the complexity of the situation to be resolved, the decision that was made split the tribe into northern and southern components.

Inasmuch as their trade at Bent's Fort was entirely in buffalo robes and horses, this increased the intensity of their raiding activities against the Kiowa and Comanche, whose northern boundary now became the Arkansas River. The Cheyenne and Arapaho, with a constant supply of arms and ammunition available, effectively controlled the Plains between the Platte and Arkansas and succeeded in containing their enemies below the latter river.

The Kiowa and Comanche, under ever increasing pressure from Indian and White enemies on the east and south, where their territory was being gradually diminished, had no regular source of guns and ammunition to resist these incursions. In this situation, without a dependable outlet for their large reserves of horses, they sued for peace with the Cheyenne and Arapaho as a necessary compromise to obtain the needed arms. The Cheyenne on their side, thus had opened to them a tremendous reservoir of horse herds in the Southwest and Mexico which they could prey upon to carry on their trade.

Change in Basic Subsistence. In viewing the course and development of Cheyenne history, it can now be seen that trade was an ever present factor, exerting its influence directly and indirectly. Despite the lack of precise historical evidence, it thus becomes possible to hypothecate the dynamics of certain changes in Cheyenne cultural history with somewhat greater lucidity, if not accuracy, by taking into account the hitherto neglected influences of trade.

The earliest historical references to the Cheyenne do not permit us even to guess at the degree to which they participated in trade, but they do point quite clearly to the fact that the Cheyenne were at least indirectly affected by certain results of the trade. Hostilities among the aborigines of the northeast, whence the Cheyenne came, were in great part engendered by contact and trade with the Europeans on the part of a number of tribes. The desire of the powerful Dakota tribes to obtain the advantages of trade in the seventeenth century were indirectly responsible for the westward movement of the Cheyenne.

The evidence indicates that the Cheyenne were settled in 1700 on the Sheyenne branch of the Red River, in North Dakota. Although they were undoubtedly bothered by Assiniboin, Cree, Chippewa, and Dakota, they also must have been engaged in trade relations with all or some of these tribes at one time or another. With the introduction of the horse after 1740 or thereabouts, on the Upper Missouri, that animal became as important as an item of trade as it was in subsistence production, and these two purposes were inextricably interwoven in the resultant quest for horses. The trade factor must have been, therefore, an important catalytic agent in the transition of the Cheyenne from a horticultural to an equestrian nomad group.

Another factor which probably affected their drift towards an equestrian nomad life was their geographical location. After 1700, they were definitely out of the northeastern forest areas, which were well under the control of other tribes east of the Red River. On the Sheyenne River they were a relatively isolated group of comparatively small population. They were out on the Plains, and were not on an important body of water so essential to European trade. Their position was tantamount to being in a cul-de-sac, off the beaten path.

The Cheyenne were, therefore, not presented with choices similar to those of the more populous horticultural villages of the Upper Missouri. The trade came to the Mandan, Hidatsa, and Arikara from the Europeans and the surrounding nomadic tribes. By the time the Cheyenne founded some villages on the Missouri, the Mandan and Hidatsa and Arikara were too well established in their horticultural and commercial activities for the Cheyenne to gain a foothold and engage in a horticultural existence equivalent to the older tribes. From the viewpoint of archaeology this may, perhaps, explain why it is so difficult to find Cheyenne sites on the Upper Missouri. Horticultural villages established there by elements of the tribe which came from the Sheyenne River of North Dakota may have been inhabited for relatively short periods of time only. Furthermore, this would have been a time of great flux and instability, a condition which would militate against the deposition of any substantial or lasting detritus.

How the Cheyenne obtained their first horses, it is impossible to tell. Although it may not have been through trade, they became more readily part of the Upper Missouri trade complex by virtue of their possession of horses; and with the passage of time they assumed the role of providers of horses to the Upper Missouri villages, in which role we see them by the beginning of the nineteenth century.

The choices which led them to assume an equestrian buffalo-hunting life were thus the result of a number of factors and events coexisting at a certain period in their history: geographical location in an area of buffalo herds relatively isolated from peoples east and west; arrival of the horse in the Upper Missouri area by 1742; their relative weakness in terms of numbers; and the fact that the Upper Missouri villages were already well established in terms of horticultural commerce. Their avenue of least resistance and greatest cultural advantage lay in the direction of equestrian nomadism, the process of change having been stimulated by the quest for horses as articles of trade.

Changes in Values and Attitudes. The institution of trade was probably a more vital factor in the cultural history of the Plains Indians than it is generally thought to have been, and further analysis of aboriginal cultures, taking this factor as a point of departure not only may shed additional light on various aspects of those cultures, but may also show the processes by means of which they underwent change.

It is well known, on the basis of archaeological evidence, that intertribal trade took place in pre-Columbian times. To what extent this trade was carried on, it is ultimately impossible to tell because conclusions in this respect rest only on the imperishable materials excavated. It is difficult to estimate the degree to which intertribal trade took place from the evidence of catlinite or obsidian alone. It is not until historic times that documentation makes us aware of the amount of food and other perishable products which were involved in the commercial transactions of aboriginal peoples. But then, the trade as we know it from documentation is no longer a reflection of the pristine aboriginal situation. From the time of arrival of Europeans on the North American mainland they became engaged in trade relations with the aborigines; and it may be said that from that time on the character of native production and exchange underwent a transformation whose full significance and ramifying effects in terms of the native cultures has perhaps to this day not been fully appreciated.

It has been pointed out that the quest for horses must be understood as a function of trade, both intertribal and European. It has also been indicated that this need for horses stimulated warfare. If we accept studies which demonstrate that in pre-Columbian times socio-religious motives dominated warfare and that the economic factor was relatively minor,[1] then it seems fairly obvious that after the efflorescence of European and intertribal trade the economic motive gained in importance. This being the case, it is not too difficult to see that the earlier rationale and beliefs might still remain attached to the more materialistic nature of the later economic motive for waging war.

Thus, in his account of the formation of the raiding party of forty-two Bow-String soldiers, later killed by the Kiowa, Grinnell states that "... a man named Hollow Hip kept talking of going to war. He said: 'Why should we not go to war ? It is a bad thing to live to be an old man. A man can die but once.' Bear Above also urged this..." On the other hand, Grinnell further states specifically with regard to this war party, that "... their intention was to go south in search of a Kiowa or Co-

[1] See Smith, 1938; Mishkin, 1940.

manche camp from which they could take horses and perhaps a few scalps. They were on foot."[2]

Of all the conversation connected with this event, we have recorded for us only the words of Hollow Hip. If other men spoke of trade and profits, or the need to replace some worn-out buffalo horses or war horses, their individual motives remain unrecorded. Only the idealistic speech of Hollow Hip has come down to us. Nevertheless, let us take strong note of the fact that these men took to the warpath with the avowed purpose of acquiring horses and only incidentally to take scalps – a project well qualified by the words "perhaps" and "few." But an important question remains unanswered by Grinnell's account. Why were these men so "anxious" to go to war to secure horses that they resorted to the extreme measure of beating the keeper of the Medicine Arrows in order to compel him to perform the renewal ceremonies without which they could not depart? An answer may be attempted in the light of some of the history considered in this paper.

The year was 1837. Approximately five years earlier, Bent's Fort had been established on the Arkansas River along the Santa Fe Trail. The Cheyenne and Arapaho were the chief Indian traders at this post, though a few other groups visited it from time to time. The Kiowa and Comanche were as yet almost completely excluded. Grinnell writes that "... as the Cheyennes and Arapahoes were constantly at Bent's in those days, the Kiowas and Comanches would not have gone to trade at a point where they would have been almost certain to meet enemies."[3] The season was summer, for the Southern Arapaho were camped with the Cheyenne and holding a Sun-Dance. Apart from the fact that the most sacred tribal ceremonies were held at this time of year, it was also, during the period we are considering, the season when the trade in horses and mules took place with Bent's traders. It was thus a period during which young, headstrong, impulsive men had special need for horses, for, as Grinnell has said, "The Indians constantly paid for their goods with these animals." Time is short for such men. The few brief months of summer must also be consumed in tribal hunts and tribal ceremonies, in addition to the trade on which they now rely for guns, ammunition, knives, and other necessaries. When, therefore, an old man, no longer able to achieve the fruits of war, whose chief concern is with ceremonial performances, tells young men in urgent need of horses that the time is inauspicious for their departure, they will violate social amenities and resort to force in order to achieve their purpose. Seen in the light of trade stimuli and requirements, the incident described by Grinnell as almost pure narrative becomes more meaningful.

[2] Grinnell, 1915, p. 43. This incident is given in detail above.
[3] *Ibid.*, p. 45.

6*

On the other hand, how far did the personality of the keeper of the
Sacred Arrows influence the decision of the soldiers to beat him up ?
Would it have happened with a stronger, more influential ceremonial
leader in the same post ? Were the soldiers taking advantage also of a
popular attitude of indifference towards Gray Thunder, the victim of
their anger ? These questions are asked in view of Gray Thunder's last
words before being killed in the battle on Wolf Creek, fought by the
Cheyenne in 1838 with the Kiowa, to avenge the death of the forty-two
Bow-string Soldiers. According to Grinnell, the Keeper of the Sacred
Arrows sought death with these words: "I will now give the people a
chance to get a smarter man to guide them. They have been calling me a
fool."[4] Was the office sacred apart from the incumbent ? Grinnell states
that the Keeper of the Sacred Arrows was ". . . in a sense, the director of
the tribe's affairs," while Eggan writes that "The ritual head of the
Cheyenne was the keeper of the sacred Medicine Arrows,. . ."[5] How can
such treatment and such a popular attitude as described here be recon-
ciled with such a sacred office ?

Historical clues provide a glimpse at popular attitudes and specific
actions which, when seen in the light of the dynamics of history, give a
clearer perspective on the interrelations of different aspects of culture.
The required ceremony was performed; but certainly not in the traditional manner, and not with the traditional attitudes. The person of the
priest was violated; he performed the ceremony under duress; the social
atmosphere was hardly sacred; the people apparently considered the
priest to be a fool. All this in connection with what Grinnell considered
to be probably the most solemn of all the Cheyenne tribal ceremonies –
a ceremony for health, prosperity, and long life in times of peace; and
for strength, protection, and victory in war.[6] We are here dealing with
the "eternal verities" of a people, not to be dismissed or changed or
affected in any society by "light or transient causes." When in a
sufficient number of instances an institution conflicts with the requirements of trade, the institution or practice may be modified, or popular
attitudes toward it may change, or the values centered around it may
be subtly influenced.

Consider the case of Yellow Wolf who ". . . seldom or never went to
war for scalps. . ." but who was outstandingly successful in capturing
horses from the Kiowa and Comanche. We saw that as leader of a war
party he refused to observe the necessary ceremonies which, if impro-
perly performed would necessitate the party's turning back. No slave of
his culture was Yellow Wolf. Weighing them in the balance, he found
that material necessity outweighed ceremonial necessity. Yellow Wolf
did much trading with the Bent brothers; he therefore needed many
horses. Could it be that this need for horses to trade was responsible for

[4] *Ibid.*, p. 56.   [5] Eggan, 1937b, p. 38.   [6] Grinnell, 1910, pp. 542—552.

the feeling that certain supernatural precautionary measures could be dispensed with on the chance that improper observance might interfere with the object of the expedition? If so, then it can only mean that men's attitudes and values were being slowly revised under the pressure of powerful external forces.

Yellow Wolf is not the only example which may be cited in this connection. There were Elk River and others. But in the case of Yellow Wolf we must note the fact that he was a chief who saw the portent of the future and he realized that the future belonged to the White man's culture and economy.[7]

If then, the factor of trade and its need for horses loomed so importantly in Plains culture, it also becomes possible to show how status was affected by the same factor. In this connection we have already cited Grinnell to the effect that men could and did build reputations as courageous and accomplished warriors purely on their skill in capturing horses from their enemies. In Grinnell's own words, "Such men went to war for the sole purpose of increasing their possessions by capturing horses; that is, they carried on war as a business – for profit."[8] And they could even boast that they had no coups or scalps to their credit. If such men could, as Grinnell says, maintain positions of respect and leadership and hold the esteem of the people, then values may have again undergone revision as a consequence of the stimulus provided by trade in the quest for horses. When men go to war *only* to take horses, pursue such an activity *only* for "business," then there must be a constant, effective, and dynamic motivation beyond mere subsistence, or replacement of animals, or desire of a reputation for generosity. It would appear that trade is just such a factor inasmuch as it was an expanding process by which the need for European articles and goods of native production, on which the Indians came to rely so heavily, was ultimately fulfilled.

[7] Witness the following statement made by Abert in his report for 1846: "(Yellow Wolf) is a man of considerable influence, of enlarged views, and gifted with more foresight than any other man in his tribe. He frequently talks of the diminishing numbers of his people, and the decrease of the once abundant buffalo. He says that in a few years they will become extinct; and unless the Indians wish to pass away also, they will have to adopt the habits of the white people, using such measures to produce subsistence as will render them independent of the precarious reliance afforded by the game. He has proposed to the interpreter at Bent's Fort, to give him a number of mules, in the proportion of one from every man in the tribe, if he would build them a structure similar to Bent's fort, and instruct them to cultivate the ground, and to raise cattle. He says that for some time his people would not be content to relinquish the delights of the chase and then the old men and squaws might remain at home cultivating the grounds, and be safely secured in their fort from the depredations of hostile tribes" (1848, p. 422).

[8] Grinnell, 1923b, Vol. 2, p. 2.

Change in the Pattern of Authority. In their trade with the Indians, Europeans for the most part, wished to deal with the people through an authority which would also be responsible for their safety. Thus, in the Central and Southern Plains, at any rate, trading with Europeans was done through the medium of chiefs or headmen. As we have seen, it was in this manner, too, that the prices were very often agreed upon. In the case of the Cheyenne, at least, it was through the chief that the presence of a trader was announced to the people who, at the same time, might be informed of the kinds of goods available and acceptable in exchange. This type of centralized authority functioned, as far as we can see, both in the band and tribal organization, for in the historical literature the nature of the social group the traveler or trader was dealing with is too often unclear.

Lewis has attempted to show that during the period of monopoly control of the fur trade the authority of Blackfoot chiefs was greatest; while after the era of intense competition the authority of the chiefs waned when European traders brought their goods to the very tipi doors of the people.[9] In the Central and Southern Plains, as among the Cheyenne and other equestrian nomads, the Indians brought their furs or other trade goods to the tipi of the chief where the business with the trader was conducted. Even where the Indians went to trade at a fort in the Plains, the chiefs were the ones who entered the establishment first to inquire about prices. In this manner, trade with Europeans would serve to reinforce the authority of the chiefs.

As we have already seen, intertribal trade was also conducted through the authority of chiefs, especially when guns and horses were involved in the exchange. Although the direct participation of the chiefs is not often mentioned in historical descriptions of ceremonial trade, their authority over such occasions may be inferred not only from the necessity of having organizers, but also from indirect references in the literature. From here it is but a short step to the making of peace between tribes, for trade purposes, through the authority of the chiefs. This was clearly indicated in the abortive peace treaty in 1806 between the Cheyenne and Hidatsa and in the great peace of 1840 between the Cheyenne and the Kiowa. We receive an impression of intertribal trade relations in the Plains reinforcing a centralized authority.

However, other changes loom as large. It is of interest to note that while in both instances there were present elements which militated against the conclusion of peace, in 1840 peace was accomplished. This was probably a result of the fact that the nature of the centralized political authority among the Cheyenne had undergone a change under the influence of trade. In 1806, the sudden arrival of the Assiniboin vitiated the peace proceedings. In 1840, peace was concluded in spite of

[9] Lewis, 1942, p. 42.

CHANGE IN THE PATTERN OF AUTHORITY

the fact that so important an event as the death of forty-two Bow-string Soldiers, killed by the Kiowa, was still unavenged. Although the Kiowa chief offered to return the scalps of the Cheyenne, the chief of the latter tribe told him to dispose of the scalps as he saw fit, for if they were brought to light they would only reopen old animosities and interfere with the peace. We see here a genuine desire to come to terms, a desire so great as to completely overshadow older values and attitudes which in the present situation were relegated to the background. Although the Cheyenne chiefs were here the conventional instrument for the making of peace, their decision, it will be remembered, was not made final without their first consulting "the strongest and the bravest" of the military societies of the day, the Dog Soldiers. Effective political control thus becomes tied up to a certain extent with the most active males organized into groups whose disciplinary and legal functions were only part of their daily round of activities. The men in the military societies were most often on the warpath for horses; these were the men who were, therefore, undoubtedly among the most active traders; and they were consequently most concerned with questions of peace and war. It would appear, then, entirely logical that the developing trade situation with its need for horses, should have been an important stimulus in the development of the authority of military societies.

While centralized authority might also be active in war, such occasions were limited, among the Cheyenne, to revenge expeditions. There have been only six recorded instances of the entire Cheyenne tribe moving against an enemy, and while loot and captives were taken in those cases, the motivation was not originally and exclusively economic.[10] Here, too, the chiefs left the decision for final action up to a military society, and it was necessary for members of such an organization to take the initiative. They visited the various bands of the tribe, created sentiment for the expedition, and arranged for all to meet at an appointed time and place, for there was not always a unanimity of opinion in behalf of this type of action.[11] Apparently, it was also customary for those interested in avenging the death of their relatives by means of tribal warfare to persuade the responsible military society through presents, primarily of horses. Once organized, such war expeditions were carried out under the aegis of the sacred tribal symbols – the Medicine Arrows and the Sacred Hat. However, economic warfare in the form of the quest for horses was always carried out on the raiding party level, and this pattern prevailed throughout the period when trade was among the most important motivations for warfare. If tribal warfare was an early pattern, as in the case of the Blackfoot,[12] it persisted only on the aforementioned level. Lewis has stated that "as a result of the introduction of the horse and

[10] Grinnell, 1915, p. 69.
[11] *Ibid.*, pp. 47, 80.
[12] Lewis, 1942, pp. 46—49.

gun and fur trade ... large massed forces under central leadership gave
way to the small raiding party..."[13] It is not possible to trace changes in
Cheyenne warfare resulting from trade situations, but it may be said
with a reasonable degree of certainty that, throughout the period
covered in this study, the raiding party prevailed in every situation
except the six cases of tribal revenge to which reference has been made.
In general, the organization, leadership, and composition of war parties,
during the period covered in the present study, is in accord with the
analysis of Plains warfare made by Smith.[14]

In the light of the broadened perspective contributed to the conventional conception of Plains culture by the evidence adduced in the
present study, it is now possible to say that all the tribal groups on the
Great Plains were participants in a trading economy which functioned
on a barter basis. The nature of this economy and its effects upon the
aboriginal cultures cannot be comprehended simply in terms of the
relations between Indian and Indian alone nor in terms of Indian and
White relations alone. Both types of trade relations were interpenetrat-
ing, interacting, and interdependent to form a total trade economy in
which people of different cultures and different historical backgrounds
were reacting to similar economic forces. Within the framework of this
trading economy there existed cultures of different basic subsistence
types (which might be viewed as technologies exploiting different
aspects of a similar environment), whose production was geared to the
requirements of trade. Although the profound influence of the horse in
the overall development of Plains culture has long since been established,
in the light of the problem considered here it was of prime importance as a
medium of exchange and as a powerful instrument of production.

It is probably true that any group pursuing, for example, a hunting or
horticultural way of life could supply itself with food exclusively on the
basis of its own production. It is also true that no group, in the Plains at
any rate, did live exclusively on the type of food which its technology
was predominantly adapted to produce. Thus hunters required products
of the soil as part of their diet, and horticulturists required products of
the hunt to satisfy their dietary needs. In the region of the Great Plains
where both types of technology existed there was a constant interchange
of goods, and consequently a supply of food beyond the needs of subsistence requirements, for purposes of trade, was a constant factor in production. This was also true of other types of goods as catalogued in the
body of this paper. If a similar situation with regard to production and
exchange existed in pre-Columbian times, then under the influence of
the horse and the fur trade, those factors were considerably intensified.
Tribal entities became so interdependent on the basis of trade as a

[13] *Ibid.*, p. 59.   [14] Smith, 1938.

method of supplying certain needs which became culturally prescribed and necessary, that it may be possible to conceive of those tribal entities as pursuing technologies which functioned within the larger framework of a trade economy. In terms of this trade economy it becomes possible to visualize a balance of diverse technologies whose production, though not geared to trade in their entirety, is sufficiently interdependent to cause widespread repercussions when any of them are affected by external factors. We thus have seen how under a variety of historical conditions trade may be influenced for either peace or war, and our discussion has shown that it engendered both.

If it is legitimate to explain the interrelationships of tribes in such terms, then the history of such a group as the Cheyenne, from the point of view of its participation in a trade economy, becomes significantly clearer, on the basis of the data already adduced. Their movement westward under the impact of forces loosed by trade, their adoption of equestrian buffalo hunting at least under the partial influence of trade, their participation in Plains life as horse traders and purchasers of agricultural produce, the enmities of the tribe in terms of competition for trade advantages, the influences for peace in terms of trade necessity, the division of the tribe on the basis of the advantages to be derived from different trading situations — all of these factors may be comprehended in terms of a far-reaching system of trade in which the Cheyenne, together with other peoples, were intertwined.

BIBLIOGRAPHY

ABEL, ANNIE HELOISE, *editor*
    1939. *Tabeau's Narrative of Loisel's Expedition to the Upper Missouri.* Norman, Oklahoma.
ABERT, LIEUTENANT J. W.
    1848. "Report of Lieut. J. W. Abert of his Examination of New Mexico in the years 1846—47." *30th Congress — First Session, Ex. Doc. No. 41,* pp. 419—546. Washington.
ATKINSON, H.
    1826. "*Movements of the Expedition which Lately Ascended the* Missouri River, etc." *19th Congress, 1st Session, Doc. 117, House of Representatives, War Department.* Washington.
BLAIR, EMMA HELEN
    1911. *The Indian Tribes of the Upper Mississippi Valley and Region of the Great Lakes.* 2 Vols. Cleveland.
BOLTON, HERBERT EUGENE
    1914. *Athanase De Mezieres and the Louisiana-Texas Frontier 1768–1780.* 2 Vols. Cleveland.
BRACKENRIDGE, H. M.
    1811. "Journal of a Voyage Up the River Missouri (in the year 1811)." Reprinted in Thwaites, 1906, Vol. 6.
BRADBURY, JOHN
    1809–1811. "Travels In the Interior of America in the Years 1809, 1810, 1811." Reprinted in Thwaites, 1906, Vol. 5.
BRANCH, E. DOUGLAS
    1929. *The Hunting of the Buffalo.* New York, London.
BRIGGS, HAROLD E.
    1940. *Frontiers of the Northwest.* New York, London.
CARVER, JONATHAN
    1778. *Travels through the Interior Parts of North America in the Years 1766, 1767, 1768.* London.
CHITTENDEN, HIRAM MARTIN
    1935. *The American Fur Trade of the Far West.* 2 Vols. New York.
CLARK, W. P.
    1885. *The Indian Sign Language.* Philadelphia.
COMFORT, A. J.
    1873. "Indian Mounds Near Fort Wadsworth, Dakota Territory." *Annual Report of the Board of Regents of the Smithsonian Institution ... for the year 1871,* pp. 389–402.
COUES, ELLIOTT, *editor*
    1897. *New Light on the Early History of the Greater Northwest: The Manuscript Journals of Alexander Henry and of David Thompson, 1799–1814.* 3 Vols. New York.
CUTLER, JERVIS
    1812. *A Topographical Description of the State of Ohio, Indiana Territory, and Louisiana ... To which is added An Interesting Journal of Mr. Chas. Le Raye ...* Boston.

DAVIDSON, GORDON CHARLES
1918. "The North West Company." *University of California Publications in History*, Vol. VII. Berkeley.
DE LAND, CHARLES E.
1906. "The Aborigines of South Dakota." (Editorial Notes by Doane Robinson). *South Dakota Historical Collections*, Vol. III, pp. 267–586.
DORSEY, GEORGE A.
1905. "The Cheyenne"
I. Ceremonial Organization. *Field Columbian Museum, Publication 99, Anthropological Series*, Vol. IX, No. 1, Chicago.
II. The Sun Dance. *Publication 103*, Vol. IX, No. 2.
EGGAN, FRED
1937a. *Social Anthropology of North American Tribes, editor*. Chicago.
1937b. "The Cheyenne and Arapaho Kinship System." *In Eggan 1937a*, pp. 33–95.
FARNHAM, THOMAS JEFFERSON
1839. "Travels In the Great Western Prairies, the Anahuac and Rocky Mountains, and In the Oregon Country." Reprinted in Thwaites, 1906, Vols. 28 & 29.
FOREMAN, GRANT
1926. *Pioneer Days In the Early Southwest*. Cleveland.
FOWLER, JACOB
1898 (?) "The Journal of Jacob Fowler, 1821–22." Vol. I *American Explorers Series*. Elliott Coues, ed. Francis P. Harper.
FREMONT, COL. JOHN CHARLES
1856. "A Narrative of the Exploring Expedition of Oregon and North California." In Smucker, p. 189ff.
GARRARD, LEWIS H.
1938. "Wah – To – Yah And the Taos Trail." Ed. by Ralph P. Bieber. *The Southwest Historical Series*, Vol. VI.
GRINNELL, GEORGE BIRD
1910. "The Great Mysteries of the Cheyenne." *American Anthropologist*, n. s., Vol. 12, pp. 542–575.
1915. *The Fighting Cheyennes*. New York.
1918. "Early Cheyenne Villages." *American Anthropologist*, Vol. 20, No. 4, pp. 359–380.
1923a. "Bent's Old Fort And Its Builders." *Collections of the Kansas State Historical Society*, Vol. XV, pp. 28–91. Topeka.
1923b. *The Cheyenne Indians, their History and Ways of Life*. 2 Vols. New Haven.
1926. *By Cheyenne Campfires*. New Haven.
HAFEN, LEROY R.
1932. "A Report from the First Indian Agent of the Upper Platte and Arkansas." *New Spain and the Anglo-American West, Historical Contributions*. Presented to Herbert Eugene Bolton. Charles W. Hackett, editor.
HAINES, FRANCIS
1938. "The Northward Spread of Horses Among the Plains Indians." *American Anthropologist*, n. s. Vol. 40, pp. 429–437.
HARMON, DANIEL WILLIAMS
1903. *Journal of Voyages and Travels in the Interior of North America*. New York.

HAXO, HENRY E., *translator*
    1941. "The Journal of La Verendrye, 1738–39." Introduction by O. G.
        Libby. *North Dakota Historical Quarterly*, Vol. 8, No. 4.
HAYDEN, F. V.
    1863. "On the Ethnography and Philology Of the Indian Tribes of the
        Missouri Valley." *Transactions of the American Philosophical Society*,
        Vol. XII, New Series, pp. 231–461. Philadelphia.
HODGE, F. W., *editor*
    1907. *Handbook of American Indians North of Mexico*. 2 Vols. Smithsonian
        Institution, Bureau of American Ethnology, Bulletin 30. Washing-
        ton.
HOSMER, JAMES KENDALL, *editor*
    1904. *Gass's Journal of the Lewis And Clark Expedition*. Chicago.
HYDE, GEORGE E.
    1937. *Red Cloud's Folk: A History of the Oglala Sioux Indians*. Norman,
        Oklahoma.
INNIS, HAROLD A.
    1930. *The Fur Trade in Canada*. New Haven.
JAMES, EDWIN
    1819. "Account of an Expedition from Pittsburgh to the Rocky Mountains,
        performed in the Years 1819, 1820 ... under the Command of
        Maj. S. H. Long." Reprinted in Thwaites, 1906, Vols. 14, 15, 16, 17,
        under the title "James' Account of S. H. Long's Expedition, 1819–
        1820."
LA ROCQUE, F. A.
    1889. "The Missouri Journal, 1804–1805." In Masson, Vol. I, pp. 299–313.
LESSER, ALEXANDER
    1933. *The Pawnee Ghost Dance Hand Game*. Columbia University Contri-
        butions to Anthropology, Vol. 16. New York.
LEWIS, OSCAR
    1942. *The Effects of White Contact Upon Blackfoot Culture, with Special
        Reference to the Role of the Fur Trade*. Monographs of the American
        Ethnological Society, VI. New York.
LLEWELLYN, K. N., and E. ADAMSON HOEBEL
    1941. *The Cheyenne Way. Conflict and Case Law In Primitive Juris-
        prudence*. Norman, Oklahoma.
LONG, MAJOR STEPHEN H.
    1860–67. "Voyage in a Six-Oared Skiff to The Falls of Saint Anthony in
        1817." *Collections of the Minnesota Historical Society*, Vol. II, pp.
        9–83.
LOWIE, ROBERT H.
    1909. "The Assiniboin." *Anthropological Papers, American Museum of
        Natural History*, Vol. 4, Part I. New York.
LUTTIG, JOHN C.
    1920. "Journal of A Fur-Trading Expedition On the Upper Missouri,
        1812–1813." Stella M. Drumm, ed., *Missouri Historical Society*. St.
        Louis.
MACKENZIE, CHARLES
    1889. "The Mississouri Indians. A Narrative of Four Trading Expeditions
        to the Mississouri 1804–1805–1806." In Masson, 1889, Vol. I, pp.
        315–393.
MACLEOD, WILLIAM CHRISTIE
    1928. *The American Indian Frontier*. New York.

MANDELBAUM, DAVID G.
    1940. "The Plains Cree." *Anthropological Papers, American Museum of Natural History*, Vol. 37, Part II, pp. 153–316. New York.
MARCY, CAPTAIN RANDOLPH B.
    1937. *Adventure On Red River*. Edited and annotated by Grant Foreman. Norman, Oklahoma.
MARGRY, PIERRE
    1879. *Découvertes et Etablissements Des Francais dans L'Quest et dans Le Sud de L'Amerique Septentrionale, 1614–1698.* Vol II. Paris.
MASSON, L. R., *editor*
    1889. *Les Bourgeois de la Compagnie du Nord-Quest.* Vol 1.
MAXIMILIAN, PRINCE OF WIED
    1832. "Travels In the Interior of North America, 1832–1834." Reprinted in Thwaites, 1906, Vols. 32–34.
McDONNELL, JOHN
    1889. "Some Account of the Red River." In Masson, Vol. I, pp. 267–281.
MEKEEL, SCUDDER
    1943. "A Short History of the Teton Dakota." *North Dakota Historical Quarterly*, Vol. X, pp. 137–205. Bismarck, N. D.
MISHKIN, BERNARD
    1940. *Rank and Warfare Among the Plains Indians.* Monographs of the American Ethnological Society, III. New York.
MOONEY, JAMES
    1898. *Calendar History of the Kiowa Indians.* Seventeenth Annual Report, Bureau of American Ethnology, 1895–96, Part I. Washington.
    1905–1907. *The Cheyenne Indians.* Memoirs of the American Anthropological Association, Vol. I, Part 6, pp. 357–442.
MORTON, ARTHUR S.
    n. d.   *A History of the Canadian West.* London.
MORSE, REV. JEDIDIAH
    1822.   *A Report to the Secretary of War, On Indian Affairs, Comprising A Narrative of a Tour Performed In the Summer of 1820 . . .* New Haven
NASATIR, ABRAHAM P.
    1927. "Jacques D'Eglise On the Upper Missouri, 1791–1795." *The Mississippi Valley Historical Review*, Vol. XIV, pp. 47–56.
NEILL, REV. EDWARD DUFFIELD
    1883. *The History of Minnesota: From the Earliest French Explorations to the Present Time.* Fifth Edition. Minneapolis.
NUTE, GRACE LEE
    1941. "Hudson's Bay Company Posts in the Minnesota Country." *Minnesota History*, Vol. XXII, pp. 270–289.
    1941.b. *The Voyageur's Highway.* St. Paul
PERRAULT, JEAN BAPTISTE
    1909. "Narrative of Travels and Adventures, 1783–1820." *Michigan Pioneer and Historical Collections*, Vol. 37, pp. 508–619. Lansing.
PERRIN DU LAC
    1807. "Travels Through the Two Louisianas in 1801, 1802, 1803." In Vol. 6 of *A Collection of Modern and Contemporary Voyages and Travels.* London.
PERROT, NICOLAS
    1911. "Memoir on the Manners, Customs and Religion of the Savages of North America." In Blair, Vol. I, pp. 23–272.

POND, PETER
1908. "Journal of Peter Pond, 1740–45." *Wisconsin Historical Collections,* Thwaites, ed., Vol. 18, pp. 314–354. Madison.
QUAIFE, MILO M., *editor*
1916. "Extracts From Capt. McKay's Journal — and Others." *Proceedings of the State Historical Society of Wisconsin,* pp. 186–210. Madison.
RICHARDSON, RUPERT NORVAL
1933. *The Comanche Barrier to South Plains Settlement.* Glendale, California.
RIGGS, STEPHEN RETURN
1893. *Dakota Grammar, Texts, and Ethnography.* Contributions to North American Ethnology, Vol. IX. Dept. of the Interior, U. S. Geographical and Geological Survey of the Rocky Mountain Region.
ROBINSON, DE LORME W., *editor*
1902. *Historical Sketch of North And South Dakota"* by William Maxwell Blackburn. South Dakota Historical Collections, Vol. I. Aberdeen, S. D.
ROBINSON, DOANE
1904. *A History of the Dakota or Sioux Indians.* South Dakota Historical Collections, Vol. II. Aberdeen, S. D.
SCOTT, HUGH LENOX
1907. "The Early History and the Names of the Arapaho." *American Anthropologist,* n. s., Vol. 9, pp. 545–560.
SMITH, MARIAN W.
1938. "The War Complex of the Plains Indians." *Proceedings of the American Philosophical Society,* Vol. 78. No. 3, pp. 425–464.
SMUCKER, SAMUEL M., *editor*
1856. *The Life of Col. John Charles Fremont, and His Narrative of Explorations And Adventures in Kansas, Nebraska, Oregon, and California.* New York and Auburn.
STEVENS, WAYNE EDSON
1926. *The Northwest Fur Trade, 1763–1800.* University of Illinois Studies in the Social Sciences, Vol. XIV, No. 3. Urbana.
STODDARD, MAJOR AMOS
1812. *Sketches, Historical and Descriptive, of Louisiana.* Philadelphia.
STRONG, WM. DUNCAN
1935. *An Introduction to Nebraska Archaeology.* Smithsonian Miscellaneous Collections, Vol. 93, No. 10. Washington, D.C.
1940. "From History to Prehistory in the Northern Great Plains." *In Essays In Historical Anthropology In North America* (Published in Honor of John R. Swanton) Smithsonian Miscellaneous Collections, Vol. 100, pp. 353–394. Washington, D.C.
SWANTON, JOHN R.
1930. "Some Neglected Data Bearing on Cheyenne, Chippewa, and Dakota History," *American Anthropologist,* n. s., Vol. 32, No. 1, pp. 156–160.
TEIT, JAMES A.
1930. "The Salishan Tribes of the Western Plateaus." *45th Annual Report, Bureau of American Ethnology,* pp. 23–396. Washington, D.C.
THWAITES, REUBEN GOLD, *editor*
1900. *The Jesuit Relations and Allied Documents,* Vol. 68. Cleveland.
1904. *Original Journals Of The Lewis and Clark Expedition 1804–1806.* 7 Vols. New York.
1906. *Early Western Travels 1748–1846.* 32 Vols. Cleveland.

TOHILL, LOUIS ARTHUR
    1928. "Robert Dickson, British Fur Trader On the Upper Mississippi."
        North Dakota Historical Quarterly, Vol. III, No. 1, pp. 5–49.
TRUDEAU, J. B.
    1914. *Trudeau's Journal*. South Dakota Historical Collections, Vol. VII,
        pp. 403–474.
TYRRELL, J. B., *editor*
    1916. *David Thompson's Narrative of his Explorations in Western America,
        1784–1812*. The Champlain Society, Toronto.
UMFREVILLE, EDWARD
    1790. *The Present State of Hudson's Bay*. London.
VERENDRYE
    1914. *The Chevalier Verendrye's Journal 1742–3*. South Dakota Historical
        Collections, Vol. VII, pp. 348–370.
WEBB, WALTER P.
    1931. *The Great Plains*. New York.
WILL, GEORGE F.
    1913–14. "The Cheyenne Indians of North Dakota." *Proceedings of the
        Mississippi Valley Historical Association*, Vol. VII, pp. 67–78.
WILL, GEORGE F., and GEORGE E. HYDE
    1917. *Corn Among the Indians of the Upper Missouri*. St. Louis.
WILLIAMSON, REV. T. S.
    1872. "Who Were the First Men?" *Minnesota Historical Society Collec-
        tions*, Vol. I, pp. 295–301. St. Paul.
    1880. "The Sioux or Dakotas." *Minnesota Historical Society Collections*,
        Vol. III, Part 3, pp. 283–294. St. Paul.
WILSON, GILBERT L.
    1924. "The Horse And The Dog in Hidatsa Culture." *Anthropological
        Papers, American Museum of Natural History*, Vol. 15, Part II,
        pp. 125–311. New York.
WISSLER, CLARK
    1914. "The Influence of the Horse in the Development of Plains Culture."
        American Anthropologist, Vol. 16, pp. 1–25.

INDEX

Adobe Fort: 66
Algonkians: 2, 23
American Fur Company: 22
ammunition: trade in, 22, 31, 40, 43, 45, 49, 55
Apache: horse raids to south, 15; peace with Cheyenne, 72; position of, 65, 66, 68; trade in captives, 24; war with Texas, 72.
Arapaho: and Arikara, 57; and Cheyenne, 16, 33, 42, 59, 60, 61, 65, 70; and Comanche, 62, 63, 70, 73f; and Kiowa, 59, 62, 63, 70, 73f; and Mandan, 51; and village tribes, 28; as skin workers, 59; other names for, 34; position of, 62f, 65, 80; supply of horses, 24, 60
archaeology: 1, 3, 81; see also Sheyenne-Cheyenne site
Arikara: and Arapaho, 57; and Cheyenne, 45, 49, 51, 53f, 57, 58; and Dakota, 51; and Hidatsa, 52; and Kiowa, 57; and Sioux, 65; as traders, 34, 37, 38; preference for prairie-turnip flour, 45; trade center, 22, 31; trade in maize, 22, 45; traders among, 7, 32f
Assiniboin: and Cheyenne, 8, 47, 49, 81; and Cree, 39; and Dakota, 4; and Hidatsa, 39, 47, 48; and Mandan, 39, 40, 41; as skin workers, 41; as traders, 37f; buffalo surround of, 20; prohibit gun in hunting, 18.
Atsena: 62
awls: trade in, 40, 45
axes: trade in, 17, 40, 45, 55
Ayavois: 3, 4

Bald-heads: 62
basketry products: trade in, 14; see also twine
beads: trade in, 17, 22, 44, 75
bear: 32; trade in skins, 33
Bear Above, Cheyenne chief: 82
Bear Tooth, Arapaho chief: 61
beaver: along Missouri, 28, 32f; trade in 17, 56; see also fur, fur trade
Bent, William: 64, 66

Bent's Fort: 35, 63, 66f, 73, 75, 79f; beginning of, 64, 65, 66, 83
berries, dried: trade in, 22
Big Bellies: 47
Big Foot, Cheyenne chief: 69
Big Man, Arikara chief: 31
Blackfoot: buffalo surround of, 20; changes due to fur trade, 11, 21, 86; introduction of horse to, 15; traders in food, 22
blankets: trade in, 35, 67, 75
bow and arrow: efficiency of, 17, 18f, 32; trade in, 12, 13, 14
Bow String soldiers: 87
British: and American rivalry, 58; and French rivalry, 6
buffalo: scarcity of, 72
buffalo robes: price of, 31; production of, 20f, 41, 59; trade in, 12, 13, 17, 31, 55, 67
buffalo surround: 19f
Bull, Arapaho chief: 73

calico: trade in, 75
camas: trade in, 13
Caninanbiches: 34, 44
canoes: used by Sioux, 9
Carver, Jonathan: 7, 9
catlinite: trade in, 13
Cayawa: 44
Chaa: 2
Chaiena: 2
Cheyenne: and Apache, 72ff; and Arapaho, 16, 59, 60, 61, 65, 70; and Arikara, 33, 42ff, 45, 49, 51, 53f, 57, 58; and Assiniboin, 8, 49; and Chippewa, 9, 44; and Comanche and Kiowa, 16, 60, 62, 63, 72ff, 68, 70, 79; and Gros Ventre, 59; and Hidatsa, 34, 35, 42ff, 45, 47, 52; and Mandan, 34, 42ff, 51, 60; and Pawnee, 16, 33; and Sioux, 8, 33, 51, 56f, 79; and village tribes, 28, 41, 79; as skin workers, 41; as traders, 34, 43; as trappers, 32; demand for garden produce, 23; division of, 60ff; history of, 1, 2–10, 78; horses among, 9f, 24, 47, 57,